W9-CLU-121

GLENCOE
WORLD HISTORY

Differentiated Instruction
for the World History
Classroom

Mc Graw Hill **Glencoe**

New York, New York   Columbus, Ohio   Chicago, Illinois   Woodland Hills, California

The McGraw·Hill Companies

 Glencoe

Send all inquiries to:
Glencoe/McGraw-Hill
8787 Orion Place
Columbus, OH 43240-4027

ISBN: 978-0-07-878244-2
MHID: 0-07-878244-9

Printed in the United States of America

1 2 3 4 5 6 7 8 9 10 079 10 09 08 07

Contents

To the Teacher

Guide to Using Differentiated Instruction for the World History Classroom

This **Differentiated Instruction for the World History Classroom** booklet accompanies the *Glencoe World History* Teacher Wraparound Edition. These strategies and activities are designed to give you additional resources to differentiate your instruction, addressing the different types of learners in your classroom. For each strategy and activity, the following information is provided to you in the outer margin:

Skill

The skill being learned or exhibited in the activity is noted. For example, students may be identifying central issues, creating a chart, conducting research, making connections, writing a dramatic scene, analyzing literature, or making a map.

Recommended Use

A recommended use for each strategy and activity is suggested—for example, Chapter Introduction, Group Practice, Section Wrap-Up, Concept Reinforcement, Independent Practice, or Guided Practice. The recommendations may help you plan the point in the lesson at which you want to have students complete the activity.

Level

To help you plan for the varying ability levels of your students, each strategy and activity is also leveled. These levels include Below Grade Level (BL), On Grade Level (OL), and Above Grade Level (AL). An additional level is noted for those activities that would be helpful for English Learners (EL).

Additional Features

This booklet also includes short, high-interest items interspersed with strategies and activities. These include *Learn More About* activities that provide skill practice in researching an event. Launching questions or activities may be included to help students connect information already learned with the new information to be researched.

People & Places and *Internet Learning* activities provide background information or Web sites to help students clarify main ideas, deepen comprehension and learn more about the biographical and geographic content of historical events.

CHAPTER 1 THE FIRST HUMANS

Key Terms and Reinforcement
Strategy and Activity

Compile a list of key terms for this chapter. Include words such as:

prehistory	*Australopithecus*	culture
archaeology	*Homo sapiens*	civilization
artifact	"out of Africa" theory	monarch
anthropology	systematic agriculture	priest
fossil	domestication	
hominid	artisan	

Ask students to complete a word web. Demonstrate for students the structure of a word web that includes the following components:

- word history
- related words
- synonyms
- antonyms
- part of speech
- dictionary definition
- original sentence using the word
- how the word relates to the chapter

As students encounter the word in the text, they should add to their word webs the sentence from the text that uses the word. Supply college-level dictionaries, thesauri, and word-origin dictionaries. Provide a model of the word web, using an hoverhead projector.

Key Terms and Reinforcement
*Independent Practice Skill: Use Word Webs to Analyze Important Terms
Recommended Use: Reinforcement*
OL

Prehistoric People
Strategy and Activity

Scientists have identified many hominids and early humans through archaeological findings and various dating techniques. Each time a new discovery is made, scientists review and possibly revise their ideas about the stages in human development. What do scientists believe the order of human development is? Help students organize the stages with humans and humanlike creatures in a chart. They should start with a hominid and follow the *Homo sapiens sapiens*, using the out-of-Africa theory.

Prehistoric People
*Creating a Chart
Recommended Use: Guided Practice*
BL

Neolithic Villages
Strategy and Activity

Have students compare the characteristics of the Çatalhüyük with the community the school is in. What similarities exist? What basic needs are supplied in both?

Neolithic Villages
*Comparing Time Periods
Recommended Use: Discussion Starter*
BL

Internet Learning
Archaeology and Anthropology Today

The following site has daily news updates about scientific research and discoveries. Students can follow links to read recently published articles on archaeological and anthropological news. The articles are from universities and other research organizations around the world. www.sciencedaily.com/news/fossils_ruins

Digging History
Conducting Research
Recommended Use:
Independent Practice
OL

Digging History

Strategy and Activity

Archaeologists have discovered artifacts and organic remains of early humans from excavating the earth. Excavating is still the technique most widely used, and it refers to the work done at a particular site over time. Digging is only part of the process. Have students research a past or current archaeological excavation. Ask them to describe the location and the processes being used. They should also record any discoveries made there.

Emergence of Civilization
Interdisciplinary Connection:
Language Arts
Skill: Analyze Literature
Recommended Use:
Team-Teaching Strategy
AL

Emergence of Civilization—An In-Depth Activity

Background

When humans settled in permanent villages, their cultures became more complex. Gradually, more complex cultures developed into a new form of human society called civilization. A civilization is a complex culture with a large number of people who share common elements. Historians have identified the six basic characteristics of civilizations: cities, government, religion, social structure, writing, and art. When social structure arose, it was based on economic power. Rulers and an upper class of priests, government officials, and warriors dominated society. Below this class was a large group of free people—farmers, artisans, and craftspeople. At the bottom was a slave class.

Strategy

Ask students to turn to page 70 in Glencoe Literature's *The Reader's Choice: World Literature* to read *The Story of the Dress that Sang* translated by A.W. Cardinall. The story is part of West African oral tradition. Early civilizations told stories for entertainment and for teaching the values of the society. These oral stories continued even after writing systems began to develop near the end of the Neolithic Age. Because this tale originated from storytelling traditions, the author is unknown. Point out to students that this folktale belongs to a particular folklore form about tricksters. Ask students if they can identify the trickster in the story.

> The chief saw that if Anansi was speaking true then verily the farm must be his. So he sent his messenger to see and the man came back and said that it was so. Then the Chameleon was asked what he had to say, and he said that he did not know anything about the path, that he always used to go there over the bushes and grass. This made the chief laugh, and he at once gave the farm to Anansi, who took all his children with him and gathered the crops.

Anansi is the trickster in many tales from the Ashanti people of West Africa. The two areas in West Africa where these Anansi tales are told developed different societies. In the north, herding and trade were the economic foundations. Along the coast, agriculture developed as the dominant economic activity.

Activities

Ask students the following questions, and then have them complete the activity below.

1. What explanation do you think the last sentence offers? *(The last sentence offers an explanation for why spiders hide from humans.)*

2. What is the dominant economic activity in this society? What is the social structure? *(Farming seems to be the main economic activity. There is a ruler, who has messengers, and beneath him are farmers. There is a definite focus on wealth and pleasing the chief.)*

3. **Writing Prompt** Ask students to recall a folktale they have heard and to write a few notes about it. Then have them share the tale aloud with the class.

CHAPTER 2

WESTERN ASIA AND EGYPT

Key Terms and Reinforcement
Strategy and Activity

Compile a list of key terms for this chapter. Include words such as:

polytheistic	dynasty	pastoral nomad
city-state	pharaoh	monotheistic
ziggurat	bureaucracy	satrapy
theocracy	vizier	satrap
cuneiform	mummification	monarchy
empire	hieroglyphics	
patriarchal	hieratic script	

Ask students to complete a word web. Demonstrate for students the structure of a word web that includes the following components:

- word history
- related words
- synonyms
- antonyms
- part of speech
- dictionary definition
- original sentence using the word
- how the word relates to the chapter

As students encounter the word in the text, they should add to their word webs the sentence from the text that uses the word. Supply college-level dictionaries, thesauri, and word-origin dictionaries. Provide a model of the word web, using an overhead projector.

Key Terms and Reinforcement
Independent Practice Skill:
Use Word Webs to Analyze
Important Terms
Recommended Use:
Reinforcement
OL

Thank the Sumerians
Strategy and Activity

The Sumerians introduced bronze, a writing system, the wheel, and a number system based on 60. Have students write an explanation of how they use some or all of these Sumerian inventions.

Thank the Sumerians
Making Connections
Recommended Use:
Classroom Assignment
BL

Water, Water Everywhere
Strategy and Activity

Organize students into small groups. Have each group create a Venn diagram comparing and contrasting the rivers of Mesopotamia with the Nile River in Egypt. How did the rivers affect each civilization? What seasonal changes did the rivers have? What benefits did the rivers provide? What disadvantages did the rivers create?

Water, Water Everywhere
Comparing and Contrasting
Recommended Use:
Group Practice
BL

Internet Learning
Ancient Laws

The following site has the translated text of the Code of Hammurabi. There are also some commentaries from early twentieth-century scholars.
www.fordham.edu/halsall/ancient/hamcode.html

Religious Tolerance
Strategy and Activity

Remind students that one of the basic characteristics of civilizations is religion (Chapter 1). Have students discuss some of the key religious changes that happened in the Egyptian civilization, the kingdom of Israel, and the Persian Empire. What was the cause of the upheavals associated with Amenhotep's religious revolution? Why did this lead to a loss of Egypt's empire? What does it mean that Judaism was a stateless religion? What other religions exist today that are "stateless"? What was Zoroastrianism? Tell students that even after practice of this religion dwindled, many of its aspects carried on in Persian culture and with modern-day Iranian peoples.

Ancient Writings—An In-Depth Activity
Background

Writing in Egypt emerged around 3000 B.C. The Greeks later called this earliest Egyptian writing hieroglyphics, meaning "priest-carvings" or "sacred writings." The hieroglyphic system of writing, which used both pictures and more abstract forms, was complex. Learning and practicing it took much time and skill. The Egyptian scribes were masters of the art of writing and also its teachers. At the age of 10, boys of the upper classes went to schools run by scribes. Training to be a scribe took many years. Students learned to read and write by copying texts. Discipline was strict, as is evident from the following Egyptian saying: "A boy's ears are on his back. He listens only when he is beaten."

Strategy

Ask students to turn to page 38 in Glencoe Literature's *The Reader's Choice: World Literature* to read "The Immortality of Writers." This Egyptian poem was taken from a textbook used by young Egyptian boys learning to be scribes. When writing began in Egypt, scribes were the only people who learned to read and write. Very early Egyptian hieroglyphs were carved in stone and written on papyrus. Most of the literature that we have today from ancient Egypt was written on rolls of papyrus. The development of a writing system impacted the growth of Egyptian civilization by allowing business transactions to be recorded, information to be exchanged without a person traveling, and a new way for people to express their creativity. "The Immortality of Writers" was written sometime in the New Kingdom, which lasted from 1567 B.C. to 1085 B.C. During this period, pharaohs built great buildings and temples to show their wealth and ensure that they would not be forgotten. Ask students if they can find a reference in this poem about the construction during the New Kingdom.

> Man decays, his corpse is dust,
> All his kin have perished;
> But a book makes him remembered,
> Through the mouth of its reciter.

Egyptians were very focused on the idea of immortality. A person who could afford the cost had his or her body mummified so that the spirit could exist in the afterlife.

Differentiated Instruction for the World History Classroom

Activities

Ask students the following questions, and then have them complete the activity below.

1. What is the main point of the poem? Do you agree with it? *(The main point is that authors and their works can live for ages through their words. Students should answer why they agree or disagree with this idea.)*

2. What makes this text a poem? *(It evokes emotion.)*

3. **Writing Prompt** Ask students to write a short poem giving their opinion about a topic and supporting it with descriptive words and words that evoke emotion.

CHAPTER 3

INDIA AND CHINA

Key Terms and Reinforcement
Strategy and Activity

Compile a list of key terms for this chapter. Include words such as:

monsoon	Buddhism	filial piety
Sanskrit	nirvana	pictographs
caste	Silk Road	ideographs
varnas	pilgrims	Confucianism
Hinduism	Vedas	Daoism
yoga	Bhagavad Gita	Legalism
reincarnation	aristocracy	regime
karma	Mandate of Heaven	censorate
dharma	Dao	

Ask students to complete a word web. Demonstrate for students the structure of a word web that includes the following components:

- word history
- related words
- synonyms
- antonyms
- part of speech
- dictionary definition
- original sentence using the word
- how the word relates to the chapter

As students encounter the word in the text, they should add to their word webs the sentence from the text that uses the word. Supply college-level dictionaries, thesauri, and word-origin dictionaries. Provide a model of the word web, using an overhead projector.

Life-Changing Technology
Strategy and Activity

Paper was developed in China under the Han dynasty. Have students think about how different their lives would be if paper did not exist. The Chinese also invented the seismograph during the Han dynasty. The ability to measure the earth's motion allows scientists to better understand earthquakes. Ask students to consider the benefits of a seismograph. Have students think about inventions that have been made during their lifetime. How have those technological changes affected their lives? Then ask students to think about possible inventions they might see in the future. Have them write down their predictions, supporting them with logic. Ask each student to share his or her predictions with the class and to give examples of how the invention or inventions would change his or her life.

Buddhism & Daoism
Strategy and Activity

Organize students into small groups. Have some groups represent Buddhism and some represent Daoism. Groups should prepare a presentation about their religion based on what they learned in Chapter 3. Tell students to create a poster for their presentation that shows some of the main beliefs and principles of their assigned religion. Encourage all group members to participate in their presentation.

Key Terms and Reinforcement
Independent Practice Skill: Use Word Webs to Analyze Important Terms
Recommended Use: Reinforcement
OL

Life-Changing Technology
Making Predictions
Recommended Use:
Classroom Assignment
OL

Buddhism & Daoism
Making a Presentation:
Recommended Use:
Group Practice
EL

Copyright © Glencoe/McGraw-Hill, a division of The McGraw-Hill Companies, Inc.

Learn More About
The Caste System

Have students use library or Internet sources to find out more about the caste system in India and how it has changed from its early days. How many castes are there today, and what is the Indian government doing to improve the status of lower-caste Indians?

Empires and Dynasties
Creating a Time Line
Recommended Use: Chapter Wrap-Up
BL

Empires and Dynasties
Strategy and Activity

Have students create two time lines on one sheet of paper. The first time line should show the time periods for the Mauryan Empire, the Kūsha Empire, and the Gupta Empire in India. The second time line should show the time periods for the Qin and Han dynasties in China. Encourage students to add other significant dates for each country, such as when Buddhism first appeared in India or when paper was developed in China.

People & Places
Wang Chong

The Han dynasty was responsible for great growth in China. The empire grew in size, population increased, technology advanced, and culture flourished. During this dynasty, a philosopher named Wang Chong introduced some very original ideas. Ask students to research some of the philosophical ideas of Chong. How were his ideas unique during this time period in China's history?

Knowledge in Verse
Interdisciplinary Connection:
Language Arts
Skill: Analyze Literature
Recommended Use:
Team-Teaching Strategy
AL

Knowledge in Verse—An In-Depth Activity
Background

Few cultures are as rich and varied as India's. Its literature reflects that. The earliest known Indian literature are the Vedas, which contain religious chants and stories. Originally passed down orally from generation to generation, the Vedas were recorded in Sanskrit after the development of writing. These early writings reveal that between 1500 and 400 B.C. India was a world of many small kingdoms. Various leaders, known as rajas (princes), had carved out small states. These kingdoms were often at war with one another as alliances shifted between them. They attacked another's fortresses and seized treasure. Not until the fourth century B.C. would a leader be able to establish a large Indian state.

Strategy and Activity

Ask students to turn to page 496 in Glencoe Literature's *The Reader's Choice: World Literature* to read a hymn from the Rig Veda. The Creation Hymn is one of many hymns found in the Rig Veda. There are four Vedas that together form a large collection of hymns and verses. The Rig Veda is the oldest and most important of these sacred writings. The Rig Veda, which means "knowledge in verse," is comprised of more than a thousand hymns, which were chanted or sung aloud during religious rituals and ceremonies. Today, these Vedic texts are sacred to the Hindu religion, making them the oldest surviving scriptures of any major world religion. Some Hindus believe that the Vedas were not written by humans, but instead were divine revelations. For scholars, the Vedas are one of the oldest examples of Indo-European language, so they are also very important for nonreligious reasons. In addition, the text provides great historical insight into the times and people of ancient India. Ask students to think about the insight the Creation Hymn gives them about ancient India.

Who really knows? Who will here proclaim it?
Whence was it produced? Whence is this creation?
The gods came afterwards, with the creation of this
universe. Who then knows whence it has arisen?

Hinduism developed and then changed over the past 3,500 years. Most Hindus today are not familiar with the text of the Rig Veda.

Activities

Ask students the following questions, and then have them complete the activity that follows.

1. What event does the hymn describe? *(the creation of the universe)*

2. "How many of your senses does the language of the hymn appeal to? Give examples. *(Stanzas one and two possibly appeal to the sense of hearing. Stanza two may also appeal to touch and to taste. Stanza three appeals to the senses of sight and touch.)*

3. **Writing Prompt** Ask students to work with a partner to create a skit that captures the story of creation based on the hymn. Encourage pairs to perform their skit for the class.

CHAPTER 4

ANCIENT GREECE

Key Terms and Reinforcement

Strategy and Activity

Compile a list of key terms for this chapter. Include words such as:

epic poem	democracy	oracle
arete	oligarchy	tragedy
polis	helot	philosophy
acropolis	ephor	Socratic Method
agora	Age of Pericles	Hellenistic Era
hoplite	direct democracy	Epicureanism
phalanx	ostracism	Stoicism
tyrant	ritual	

Ask students to complete a word web. Demonstrate for students the structure of a word web that includes the following components:

- word history
- related words
- synonyms
- antonyms
- part of speech
- dictionary definition
- original sentence using the word
- how the word relates to the chapter

As students encounter the word in the text, they should add to their word webs the sentence from the text that uses the word. Supply college-level dictionaries, thesauri, and word-origin dictionaries. Provide a model of the word web, using an overhead projector.

Key Terms and Reinforcement
Independent Practice Skill: Use Word Webs to Analyze Important Terms
Recommended Use: Reinforcement
OL

Athens Versus Sparta

Strategy and Activity

Assign half the class to represent Sparta and the other half to represent Athens. Each student should be firmly convinced of the superiority of his or her way of life. Have students create a brochure describing the life in either Athens or Sparta with the goal of persuading the reader that their city is the greatest in Greece. The brochures should include the best aspects of Athenian and Spartan life. Remind students that a persuasive marketing piece makes everything sound good, even the less attractive aspects. Have students present their brochures, alternating between "Athenians" and "Spartans."

Athens Versus Sparta
Writing a Persuasive Brochure
Recommended Use:
Independent Practice
OL

Learn More About
The Olympics

Have students use library or Internet sources to find out more about the history of the Olympic Games. How did these events begin as a religious festival and end up an international event blending sport and culture?

Greek Philosophy

Strategy and Activity

Help students form small groups. Assign each group one of the three great Greek philosophers. Group members will work together to answer the following questions based on the philosopher they have. How did your philosopher believe people learned? What did your philosopher think about authority or government? For what is your philosopher most famous?

People & Places
Macedon

The kingdom in the northern part of ancient Greece was called Macedon, or Macedonia. After Philip II gained control of all Greece, he was assassinated, and his son, Alexander the Great, continued this leadership, taking control of the Persian Empire and Egypt. After the Hellenistic Era ended with the defeat by Romans, Macedon became the Roman province of Macedonia around 146 B.C. When the Roman Empire split in two, Macedonia became a part of the Byzantine Empire, or Eastern Roman Empire. Today, the term *Macedonia* refers to an area somewhat unrelated to the ancient Macedon kingdom. The area includes parts of Greece, Bulgaria, the Republic of Macedonia, and Serbia.

The Moral of the Story—An In-Depth Activity

Background

Slavery was common in ancient Greece. Most people in Athens—except the very poor—owned at least one slave. The very wealthy might own large numbers. Those who did usually employed them in industry. Most often, slaves in Athens worked in the fields or in the homes as cooks and maids. Some slaves were owned by the state and worked on public construction projects.

Strategy

Ask students to turn to page 250 in Glencoe Literature's *The Reader's Choice: World Literature* to read "The Dog and the Wolf" by Aesop. Aesop is thought to be the author of many Greek fables. There is no solid proof, though, that he existed. Most biographical descriptions of Aesop state that he was a slave who told stories in sixth-century-B.C. Greece. Regardless, various collections of fables with morals are grouped as "Aesop's fables." The first collection of Aesop's fables was produced by Demetrius Phalareus, an Athenian politician during the fourth century B.C. All the Aesop's fables have a moral to the story. The values from these fables were used in ancient Greece by politicians giving speeches. Fables are popular in many cultures, and they often are told to teach religious or moral principles. Many common sayings originated from the Aesop fables, and these morals are often stated directly at the end of the story as seen in "The Dog and the Wolf":

"Better starve free than be a fat slave."

Have students think about similar phrases that they have heard and consider if they might have originated from a fable.

Activities

Ask students the following questions, and then have them complete the activity below.

1. Why do you think a slave might have told this story? *(A slave might be struggling with the thought of his or her position in life. On one hand, it is good to receive food and shelter. However, the price is very high since he or she has no freedom and can never become anything other than a slave.)*

2. Which animal was kept captive? Which life would you rather? *(The dog was kept chained up at night by his master. Answers will vary.)*

3. **Writing Prompt** Give students a few common moral phrases, such as "A man is known by the company he keeps," "An ounce of prevention is worth a pound of cure," and "Quality is better than quantity," and ask them to choose one. Then have them write a short fable to teach that moral lesson.

CHAPTER 5

ROME AND THE RISE OF CHRISTIANITY

Key Terms and Reinforcement

Strategy and Activity

Compile a list of key terms for this chapter. Include words such as:

republic	dictator	clergy
patrician	imperator	laity
plebeian	paterfamilias	plague
consul	*insulae*	inflation
praetor	procurator	
triumvirate	New Testament	

Ask students to complete a word web. Demonstrate for students the structure of a word web that includes the following components:

- word history
- related words
- synonyms
- antonyms
- part of speech
- dictionary definition
- original sentence using the word
- how the word relates to the chapter

As students encounter the word in the text, they should add to their word webs the sentence from the text that uses the word. Supply college-level dictionaries, thesauri, and word-origin dictionaries. Provide a model of the word web, using an overhead projector.

Roman Rule

Strategy and Activity

Have students use library and Internet sources to help them create a map of the Roman Empire during the Pax Romana. Have students draw or photocopy a current map of the Western Hemisphere. Then have them color in or highlight the area that was part of the Roman Empire during the 100 years of Roman Peace.

Latin Influence

Strategy and Activity

Latin was the formal language of the Roman Republic and Empire. This language is part of the Indo-European language family and belongs to the Italic group. Latin spread throughout the same areas that the Romans conquered. Many words that are used in the English language were influenced by Latin. Have students look at the word webs that they created with Chapter 5 vocabulary. Which words have a Latin origin? Ask students to work with a partner to create sentences using those words.

Key Terms and Reinforcement
Independent Practice
Skill: Use Word Webs to Analyze Important Terms
Recommended Use:
Reinforcement
OL

Roman Rule
Creating a Map
Recommended Use: Enrichment
AL

Latin Influence
Making Connections
Recommended Use: Enrichment
EL

Copyright © Glencoe/McGraw-Hill, a division of The McGraw-Hill Companies, Inc.

ROME AND THE RISE OF CHRISTIANITY

The Rise and Fall of the Roman Empire
Create a Time Line
Recommended Use:
Chapter Wrap-Up
BL

The Rise and Fall of the Roman Empire
Strategy and Activity

Have students produce a time line representing the rise and fall of the Roman Empire. The time line will be divided into nine time periods: the Expansion of the Roman Republic, the Roman State, the Roman Conquest of the Mediterranean, the End of the Republic, the Age of Augustus, the Pax Romana, the Rise of Christianity, the Reforms of Diocletian and Constantine, and the Fall of the Roman Empire. Students should color code each period and enter dates of significant events for each.

The Roman Empire's Decline
Staging a Debate
Recommended Use:
Group Practice
OL

The Roman Empire's Decline
Strategy and Activity

Organize students into small groups. Assign each group with a theory for the decline and fall of the Roman Empire. Groups should research the facts supporting their assigned theory. Have students gather information that they can use in a staged debate. Allow each group an opportunity to present its case and to respond to queries and criticisms.

People & Places
Spartacus

The famous gladiator Spartacus has been depicted in modern media numerous times. There are films, novels, video games, songs, and television shows with Spartacus as a character. In 2004 a historical novel about Spartacus was made into a television movie. Even though Spartacus did not start the revolt with the intention of making a social statement, people remember the rebellion as a revolutionary fight for the oppressed.

Knowledge in Verse—An In-Depth Activity

Background

As Roman emperors grew more powerful, many became corrupt. Nero, for example, had people killed if he wanted them out of the way, including his own mother. Without troops, the senators were unable to oppose his excesses, but the Roman legions finally revolted. Nero, abandoned by his guards, committed suicide after allegedly uttering the final words: "What an artist the world is losing in me." After Nero's death, a civil war broke out in A.D. 69. It soon became obvious that the Roman Empire had a major flaw. Without a system for selecting a new emperor, emperors could be made and deposed by the Roman legions.

Strategy

Ask students to turn to page 392 in Glencoe Literature's *The Reader's Choice: World Literature* to read *The Burning of Rome* from the *Annals* by Tacitus, translated by Michael Grant. Tacitus was eight years old when so much of Rome burned to the ground. He studied in Rome when he was a young man and grew up to write many historical works. These works have provided generations since with great insight into the times of the Roman Empire. Because Tacitus wrote in Latin, *The Burning of Rome* has been translated so that many people can learn from his vivid depiction of the actual fire and its aftermath. Ask students if they have ever had to translate something. Have a volunteer describe the challenges of translating other people's words. Point out how the word *circus* could easily be misinterpreted during the translation.

> Now started the most terrible and destructive fire which Rome had ever experienced. It began in the Circus, where it adjoins the hills. Breaking out in shops selling inflammable goods, and fanned by the wind, the conflagration instantly grew and swept the whole length of the Circus. There were no walled mansions or temples, or any other obstructions which could arrest it.

The fire destroyed many of Rome's districts and Nero's palace.

Activities

Ask students the following questions and have them complete the activities below.

1. What positive effects did the fire have on Rome? *(The areas that were rebuilt were planned and made safer. In addition, Nero built a beautiful new palace.)*

2. What description by Tacitus was most vivid for you? *(Answers will vary.)*

3. **Writing Prompt** Ask students to interview a member of their family about a memory they have of a historical or personal event. Have students listen to the historical story and then write it down, using descriptive words to create a vivid depiction.

Knowledge in Verse
Interdisciplinary Connection: Language Arts
Skill: Analyze Literature
Recommended Use:
Team-Teaching Strategy
AL

THE WORLD OF ISLAM

Key Terms and Reinforcement
Strategy and Activity

Compile a list of key terms for this chapter. Include words such as:

sheikh	caliph	bazaar
Allah	jihad	dowry
Quran	Shia	astrolabe
Islam	Sunni	minaret
Hijrah	vizier	muezzin
hajj	sultan	arabesques
shari'ah	mosque	

Ask students to complete a word web. Demonstrate for students the structure of a word web that includes the following components:

- word history
- related words
- synonyms
- antonyms
- part of speech
- dictionary definition
- original sentence using the word
- how the word relates to the chapter

As students encounter the word in the text, they should add to their word webs the sentence from the text that uses the word. Supply college-level dictionaries, thesauri, and word-origin dictionaries. Provide a model of the word web, using an overhead projector.

Key Terms and Reinforcement
*Independent Practice Skill: Use Word Webs to Analyze Important Terms
Recommended Use: Reinforcement
OL*

Monotheism
Strategy and Activity

Ask students what Judaism and Christianity have in common. Then explain that Islam is also a monotheistic religion. Muslims believe that there is only one true God. They worship the same God that Jews and Christians do. In monotheistic belief, God created the universe and is a continued presence. Ask students which monotheistic religion is the oldest. Explain that Christianity and Islam also have Abraham as part of their sacred origins. Christianity began to develop in A.D. 1, and Islam in A.D. 622.

Monotheism
*Making Connections
Recommended Use: Guided Practice
BL*

The First Crusade
Strategy and Activity

Organize students into two groups for making presentations about the First Crusade. Have one group represent the European forces and the other represent the Seljuk Turks. Groups should prepare a presentation about their side of the conflict based on what they have learned in Chapter 6 and from outside research. Instruct students to prepare their presentations with an open mind and consider the opposing viewpoint.

The First Crusade
*Making a Presentation
Recommended Use:
Group Practice
OL*

Internet Learning
Islam

The following site has information about the Islamic faith and culture. There is also an interactive time line that has faith, politics, culture, and innovation categories.
www.pbs.org/empires/islam

Sunni and Shia Muslims
Writing an Essay
Recommended Use:
Concept Introduction
AL

Sunni and Shia Muslims
Strategy and Activity

The Shia Muslims accept only the descendents of Ali as the true rulers of Islam. The Sunni Muslims accepted the Umayyads as rulers. Ask students to write an essay that describes how the split of Islam into two groups has affected history. They can either focus on a particular occurrence or write an overview. Inform them that the essay must go beyond the information provided in their textbook. Encourage them to use library and Internet sources about past and current events.

The Sacred Poetry of the Quran
Interdisciplinary Connection:
Language Arts
Skill: Analyze Literature
Recommended Use:
Team-Teaching Strategy
AL

The Sacred Poetry of the Quran
Background

The holy book of the religion of Islam is the Quran. It contains the ethical guidelines and laws by which the followers of Allah are to live. Those who practice the religion of Islam are called Muslims. Muslim scholars developed a law code knows as the *shari'ah*. It provides believers with a set of practical laws to regulate their daily lives. It is based on scholars' interpretations of the Quran and the example set by Muhammad in his life. The *shari'ah*. applies the teachings of the Quran to daily life. It regulates all aspects of Muslim life including family life, business practice, government, and moral conduct. The *shari'ah*. does not separate religious matters from civil or political law.

Strategy

Ask students to turn to page 449 in Glencoe Literature's *The Reader's Choice: World Literature* to read two verses from the Quran, as translated by N. J. Dawood. Point out to students the practical emphasis given in "The Exordium," or introduction to the Quran:

> Guide us to the straight path,
> The path of those whom You have favored,
> Not of those who have incurred Your wrath,
> Nor of those who have gone astray.

Have students read "Daylight," first silently and then aloud. Ask them to consider it as a poem meant to give practical guidance, such as in the last line:

> Therefore do not wrong the orphan, nor chide away the beggar . . .

Ask students to analyze the language of "Daylight" in terms of how it might teach people to live a better life. What is the purpose of its use of word such as *orphan, shelter, error, guide, poor,* and *enrich*? Explain that religious texts often function as powerful means of social reform.

Activities

Ask students the following questions, and then have them complete the activity below.

1. How would you summarize the main idea put forth in "The Exordium"? (Allah is kind and forgiving and therefore should be praised. People should worship only him and ask for his help to make ethical choices.)

2. What ethical guideline or law is found in "Daylight"? ("Daylight" might be interpreted to imply that one should treat others with compassion, as Allah has treated them.)

3. **Writing Prompt** Have students use library and Internet resources to learn about the Muslim observance of Ramadan. When does it occur? Ask students to investigate the meaning of Ramadan and what Muslims do to celebrate it. Have students write a short essay describing the importance of Ramadan in Islamic culture.

CHAPTER 7

EARLY AFRICAN CIVILIZATIONS

Key Terms and Reinforcement

Strategy and Activity

Compile a list of key terms for this chapter. Include words such as:

plateau	stateless society	diviner
savanna	lineage group	griot
subsistence farming	matrilineal	
Swahili	patrilineal	

Ask students to complete a word web. Demonstrate for students the structure of a word web that includes the following components:

- word history
- related words
- synonyms
- antonyms
- part of speech
- dictionary definition
- original sentence using the word
- how the word relates to the chapter

As students encounter the word in the text, they should add to their word webs the sentence from the text that uses the word. Supply college-level dictionaries, thesauri, and word-origin dictionaries. Provide a model of the word web, using an overhead projector.

Knowledge Transfer

Strategy and Activity

Trade with the Kingdom of Ghana and other parts of the world was time-consuming. Traveling through the desert, products would take 40 to 60 days to reach their trade destination. How did this affect the value of the items being traded? Help students understand how this differs in a world where you might have luxury items priority shipped in four days or possibly even overnight from the United States to Ghana. Ask students how this change affects the transmittal of cultures and ideas. Compare it to the effect trade had on the transfer of knowledge in the early history of West Africa.

> ### Learn More About
> #### Early Chroniclers of African History and Culture
>
> Early African civilizations had no written language. They maintained their histories orally. Some Arabic traders and travelers wrote about the many facets of African culture. Have students use library or Internet sources to find out more about the people who reported on early African culture and history. The text mentions two chroniclers—Ibn Battuta and Al-Bakri. Ask students if they can find others who wrote firsthand accounts about this undocumented culture.

Key Terms and Reinforcement
Independent Practice Skill:
Use Word Webs to Analyze
Important Terms
Recommended Use:
Reinforcement
OL

Knowledge Transfer
Comparing Time Periods
Recommended Use:
Discussion Starter
BL

African Diviners and Greek Oracles
Comparing and Contrasting
Recommended Use:
Concept Reinforcement
OL

African Diviners and Greek Oracles
Strategy and Activity

Have students create a two-column table on a sheet of paper. Have them write "Greek Oracle" at the top of the first column and "African Diviners" at the top of the other column. Have students compare and contrast the oracles of ancient Greece to the diviners of early Africa. Encourage students to research the topic online or at the library. After completion, student tables can be used during a class discussion comparing the religions of ancient Greece and Africa.

People & Places
Muyaka bin Haji al-Ghassaniy

The Swahili language was communicated orally since before A.D. 200. It has only been written down over the last few hundred years. One of the first written Swahili poets was Muyaka bin Haji al-Ghassaniy. Ghassaniy was born in Kenya in 1776. He is known as a composer of quatrains. A quatrain is a poem with four lines of verse. He wrote on a variety of subjects from love to philosophy.

Swahili Culture
Interdisciplinary Connection:
Language Arts
Skill: Analyze Literature
Recommended Use:
Team-Teaching Strategy
AL

Swahili Culture—An In-Depth Activity
Background

As time passed, a mixed African-Arabian culture, eventually known as Swahili, began to emerge throughout the coastal area. Intermarriage was common among the ruling groups. Gradually, the Muslim religion and Arabic architectural styles became part of a society that was still largely African.

The term *Swahili* (from sahel, meaning "coast" in Arabic, and thus "peoples of the coast") was also applied to the major language used in the area. The Swahili language arose as a result of trade between people who lived along Africa's eastern coast. The language incorporated words from both Bantu and Arabic. It enabled these two groups of people without a common language to communicate and trade. As Arabic trade in ivory and slaves spread to the north and west, the Swahili language spread there too.

Strategy

Ask students to turn to page 52 in Glencoe Literature's *The Reader's Choice: World Literature* to read the Swahili love poetry translated by Ali Ahmed Jahadhmy. Swahili poetry has flourished in the last three centuries. It is popular among the Swahili people. In fact, it is so popular that it has its own section in Swahili-language newspapers. New poems will often slip old verse into their poems. Because of the heavy Islamic influence, most of the poetry is religious in nature. However, some of it is secular. The poetry does lose some of its flavor and beauty with the translation since its verse is so complex and stylish. Swahili love poems can be recited or sung.

I do not feel ashamed
to follow you wherever you are.
Illness tortures me,
the medicine for it is your appearance.
By God, I do not find it hard
to suffer for your sake.

Activities

Ask students the following questions, and then have them complete the activity below.

1. What analogy is used in the first poem? *(medicine for an illness is related to the appeasement of a lover's presence to remove sadness)*

2. Which poem do you like the most or least? Explain why. *(Answers will vary.)*

3. **Writing Prompt** Ask students to work in groups to create their own page of poems in a newspaper. Tell them that the poems should commemorate an occurrence or special occasion. The event can be as important as buying a new house or as common as eating corn flakes for breakfast. Encourage groups to photocopy or print multiple copies of their poems to share with the entire class.

CHAPTER 8

THE ASIAN WORLD

Key Terms and Reinforcement
Strategy and Activity

Compile a list of key terms for this chapter. Include words such as:

scholar-gentry	Bushido	Mahayana
dowry	shogun	archipelago
khanate	daimyo	agriculture society
neo-Confucianism	Shinto	trading society
porcelain	Zen	
samurai	Theravada	

Ask students to complete a word web. Demonstrate for students the structure of a word web that includes the following components:

- word history
- related words
- synonyms
- antonyms
- part of speech
- dictionary definition
- original sentence using the word
- how the word relates to the chapter

As students encounter the word in the text, they should add to their word webs the sentence from the text that uses the word. Supply college-level dictionaries, thesauri, and word-origin dictionaries. Provide a model of the word web, using an overhead projector.

Key Terms and Reinforcement
Independent Practice Skill: Use Word Webs to Analyze Important Terms
Recommended Use: Reinforcement
OL

Connecting Cultures
Strategy and Activity

China, Japan, and Korea all have distinct histories and cultures. Yet, they all have had an impact on one another given their geographical location and level of contact with one another. Divide students into groups and assign each group one of the following charts: Similarities and Differences Between Chinese and Japanese History and Culture, Similarities and Differences Between Korean and Japanese History and Culture, Similarities and Differences Between Korean and Chinese History and Culture. Encourage students to use their textbook and outside sources, if necessary, to fill in the chart. Once they have finished this assignment, have each group give a presentation based on its chart.

Connecting Cultures
Creating a Chart
Recommended Use:
Group Practice
OL

Eastern Religions
Strategy and Activity

Assign students one of the following topics: Confucianism, Neo-Confucianism, Shinto, Zen Buddhism, Theravada Buddhism, Mahayana Buddhism, and Hinduism. Topics can be combined in order to compare, for example, Theravada Buddhism with Mahayana Buddhism. Students should use library or Internet sources for their research. Instruct students to write a brief one-page report about their topic.

Eastern Religions
Conducting Research
Recommended Use: Writing Assignment
AL

Learn More About
Eastern Religions and Art

Have students visit the Metropolitan Museum of Art online at www.metmuseum.org. Encourage them to browse the site, but ask them to pay special attention to the Timeline of Art History (www.metmuseum.org/toah/intro/atr/01sm.htm). They can focus on the dates that Chapter 8 covers (500–1500) and select one of the many areas in Asia to see how art was affected by that time period in history.

Leading Role
Writing a Dramatic Scene
Recommended Use: Chapter Wrap-Up
BL

Leading Role
Strategy and Activity

Organize students into groups of three or more. Help them choose a leader to depict in a dramatic scene. The leader can be from any of the many dynasties, empires, or political units, such as Tang, Sui, or Mongol, mentioned in Chapter 8. Based on the information in the text, each group will write a brief dramatic scene involving a leader. Encourage students to be creative. Allow time for each group to perform its scene.

People & Places
Miyamoto Musashi

There were many great samurai throughout Japanese history and legend. Musashi was one of the greatest swordsmen in the history of Japan. He was also an accomplished artist of sumi-e, or ink painting. His paintings are noted for their simplicity and economic use of brush stroke with a powerful effect. The famous *Samurai Trilogy* starring Toshirô Mifune and directed by Hiroshi Inagaki tells the story of Musashi's life.

Japanese Culture
Interdisciplinary Connection:
Language Arts
Skill: Analyze Literature
Recommended Use:
Team-Teaching Strategy
AL

Japanese Culture—An In-Depth Activity
Background

During much of the history of early Japan, aristocratic men believed that prose fiction was merely "vulgar gossip" and was thus beneath them. Consequently, from the ninth to the twelfth centuries, women were the most productive writers of prose fiction in Japanese. From this tradition appeared one of the world's great novels, *The Tale of Genji*. The novel was written by court author Murasaki Shikibu around the year 1000. Her novel traces the life of the nobleman Genji. Various aspects of Genji's personality are explored as he moves from youthful adventures to a life of compassion in his later years.

Strategy

Ask students to turn to page 613 in Glencoe Literature's *The Reader's Choice: World Literature* to read The Pillow Book by Sei Shōnagon. Shōnagon was a lady-in-waiting for the empress Sadako during the Heian period (784–1185). The Pillow Book is a personal diary that contains lists, personal thoughts, and gossip revolving around court life. It is brought to life with Shōnagon's gift for verse.

An elderly person warms the palms of his hands over a brazier and stretches out the wrinkles. No young man would dream of behaving in such a fashion; old people can really be quite shameless. I have seen some dreary old creatures actually resting their feet on the brazier and rubbing them against the edge while they speak. These are the kind of people who in visiting someone's house first use their fans to wipe away the dust from the mat and, when they finally sit on it, cannot stay still but are forever spreading out the front of their hunting costume or even tucking it up under their knees. One might suppose that such behavior was restricted to people of humble station; but I have observed it in quite well-bred people, including a Senior Secretary of the Fifth Rank in the Ministry of Ceremonial and a former Governor of Suruga.

Murasaki Shikibu, the author mentioned in the passage under "Background," was a court rival of Shōnagon. Shikibu, like Shōnagon, was a court lady of the empress Joto Mon'in.

Activities

Ask students the following questions, and then have them complete the activity that follows.

1. Why didn't men of early Japan write prose fiction? *(Sei Shōnagon wrote about gossip and things personal to her life much the way bloggers do.)*

2. How is the work of Sei Shōnagon similar to many of the today's bloggers? *(Because gold is all that touches this woman and is a commodity that is out of the reach of most common men, it is unrealistic for the boatmen to think they could actually touch her.)*

3. **Writing Prompt** Help students choose a partner to write about. Then instruct each student to write a daily journal for one week that revolves around both his or her life and the life of the partner. Tell students that their writing should not be inappropriate or mean-spirited.

CHAPTER 9

EMERGING EUROPE AND THE BYZANTINE EMPIRE

Key Terms and Reinforcement
Strategy and Activity

Compile a list of key terms for this chapter. Include words such as:

wergild	abbess	common law
ordeal	feudalism	Magna Carta
bishopric	vassal	Parliament
pope	knight	estate
monk	fief	patriarch
monasticism	feudal contract	schism
missionary	tournament	Crusades
nun	chivalry	infidel

Ask students to complete a word web. Demonstrate for students the structure of a word web that includes the following components:

- word history
- related words
- synonyms
- antonyms
- part of speech
- dictionary definition
- original sentence using the word
- how the word relates to the chapter

As students encounter the word in the text, they should add to their word webs the sentence from the text that uses the word. Supply college-level dictionaries, thesauri, and word-origin dictionaries. Provide a model of the word web, using an overhead projector.

Key Terms and Reinforcement
Independent Practice Skill: Use Word Webs to Analyze Important Terms Recommended Use: Reinforcement
OL

Divine Intervention
Strategy and Activity

In Germanic law, guilt or innocence was often determined by the ordeal. A physical test using fire or water was usually used to judge an accused person. If the accused person survived the physical test, then they were determined innocent. The accused might be weighted down and thrown in water. If the accused sank, he or she was guilty. If somehow the accused floated, then it was assumed that God or a supernatural power got involved to save the innocent person. The outcome of trials that involved holding a red-hot iron were usually determined several days later when the wound was inspected. If the wound was healing, then a higher power had intervened. If the wound was infected, then the person was determined guilty. Many other cultures, such as Indian and West African, also practiced similar trials. Ask students to think about the practice of using the ordeal. Have them write an essay expressing whether they agree or disagree with using the ordeal. You can extend this activity by presenting a scenario to which students could relate. The scenario should include an innocent person who is judged using a physical trial that is impossible to complete without being unharmed. Another option is to have small groups develop and perform skits that shows the unfairness of the ordeal.

Divine Intervention
Identifying Central Issues Recommended Use:
Classroom Assignment
BL

The Magna Carta
Strategy and Activity

The Magna Carta states: "No free man shall be arrested or imprisoned . . . except by the lawful judgment of his peers or by the law of the land." The Fifth Amendment to the Constitution of the United States reads: "Nor shall [any person] be deprived of life, liberty, or property without due process of law." Due process of law establishes limits to the powers of government. Although the Magna Carta primarily guaranteed rights to the English nobility, some historians believe that it also set a precedent for the U.S. Constitution. Ask students to write an essay that either supports or opposes this belief, using examples from both documents. (The National Archives Web site at www.archives.gov has a transcription of the U.S. Constitution and a translation of the complete text of the Magna Carta.) You might wish to extend this activity further by staging a class debate on the issue.

Internet Learning
Crusades

An international scholarly society for military history in the Middle Ages has a Web site (www.deremilitari.org/resources/categories/crusades1.htm) with links to many primary sources on the Crusades.

A Noble Army
Strategy and Activity

Throughout history, armies have been made up of different types of people. In ancient Rome, the army consisted mainly of well-trained professional soldiers. In the nineteenth century, Napoleon introduced the concept of forced military duty. This was a mandatory duty for men to fulfill. They became trained soldiers for the state. Another type of army is the civilian army. Civilian soldiers volunteer to protect the state. During the Middle Ages, armies consisted of knights that made a contractual agreement with a noble. The knights fought for their noble lord. Have students research a topic about knights. They can focus on anything that interests them, from the armor knights wore to the concept of chivalry. Ask students to present their research to the class.

Carolingian Empire—An In-Depth Activity
Background

During his long rule from 768 to 814, Charlemagne greatly expanded the Frankish kingdom and created what came to be known as the Carolingian Empire. At its height, this empire covered much of western and central Europe. Not until Napoleon Bonaparte's time in the nineteenth century would an empire its size be seen again in Europe. In the ninth and tenth centuries, western Europe was beset by a wave of invasions. The Muslims attacked the southern coasts of Europe and sent raiding parties into southern France. The Magyars, a people from western Asia, moved into central Europe at the end of the ninth century, settled on the plains of Hungary, and invaded western Europe.

Strategy

Ask students to turn to page 790 in Glencoe Literature's *The Reader's Choice: World Literature* to read *The Song of Roland,* translated by Frederick Goldin. The French title is *La Chanson de Roland.* This epic poem is based on an insignificant event that happened during Charlemagne's rule. In the style of an epic poem, this narrative tells of a hero's adventures. The story originated as an oral account and was not written until approximately 300 years after the actual event took place. There is a mixture of myth and historical fact in the story. The small army of Christian Basques involved in the actual historical event were changed in the epic poem into 400,000 Arab Muslims (referred to as "pagans," or "Saracens"). Roland himself was an actual historical person, but he was neither Charlemagne's nephew nor the army's most valiant chieftain, as portrayed in *The Song of Roland.*

High are the hills, and high, high are the trees;
there stand four blocks of stone, gleaming of marble.
Count Roland falls fainting on the green grass,
and is watched, all this time, by a Saracen:
who has feigned death and lies now with the others,
has smeared blood on his face and on his body;
and quickly now gets to his feet and runs—
a handsome man, strong, brave, and so crazed with pride
that he does something mad and dies for it:
laid hands on Roland, and on the arms of Roland,
and cried: "Conquered! Charles's nephew conquered!
I'll carry this sword home to Arabia!"
As he draws it, the Count begins to come round.

Activities

Ask students the following questions, and then have them complete the activity below.

1. What did Roland want to prevent happening to Durendal? *(He did not want it to get in the hands of pagans.)*

2. Why do you think the enemy in this epic poem was rewritten to be Arab Muslims? *(At the time this epic poem was written, Arab Muslims had been a long-time French enemy.)*

3. **Writing Prompt** Ask students to research the actual event (the battle at Roncevaux) on which *The Song of Roland* was based on. Have them write an essay comparing the historical facts with the epic poem's details

CHAPTER 10

EUROPE IN THE MIDDLE AGES

Key Terms and Reinforcement

Strategy and Activity

Compile a list of key terms for this chapter. Include words such as:

carruca	apprentice	theology
manor	journeymen	scholasticism
serfs	masterpiece	vernacular
money economy	lay investiture	*chanson de geste*
commercial capitalism	interdict	anti-Semitism
bourgeoisie	sacraments	new monarchies
patricians	heresy	*taille*
guilds	relics	

Ask students to complete a word web. Demonstrate for students the structure of a word web that includes the following components:

- word history
- related words
- synonyms
- antonyms
- part of speech
- dictionary definition
- original sentence using the word
- how the word relates to the chapter

As students encounter the word in the text, they should add to their word webs the sentence from the text that uses the word. Supply college-level dictionaries, thesauri, and word-origin dictionaries. Provide a model of the word web, using an overhead projector.

Key Terms and Reinforcement
Independent Practice Skill: Use Word Webs to Analyze Important Terms Recommended Use: Reinforcement OL

Roman Versus Medieval Development

Strategy and Activity

Inform students that one criterion used by geographers to differentiate between "developed" and "developing" countries is the people's ability to control their environment and to use technology to maximize the use of resources. Tell students to think about how this description applied to medieval Europe and the earlier Roman Empire. Students should choose one of these and write an essay that argues whether this civilization could be considered "developed" or "developing." Students should also consider how the physical environment, natural resources, and culture influence a civilization's development.

Roman Versus Medieval Development
Writing an Essay Recommended Use: Chapter Introduction AL

Internet Learning

Ancient Laws

The following site has images of early and high gothic architecture.
www.bc.edu/bc_org/avp/cas/fnart/arch/gothic_arch.html

Relationship Obligations

Comparing Time Periods
Recommended Use: Discussion Starter
AL

Relationship Obligations

Strategy and Activity

Have students compare the relationship of serfs and lords with the relationship of citizens and the U.S. government. What kinds of taxes are paid? What kinds of protection are provided?

> ## Learn More About
> **Serfdom**
>
> Serfs were bound to the land of their lord. They could not leave without permission, and their children inherited the position of serfdom. In many relationships, lords had a variety of legal rights over their serfs. Some serfs had to obtain approval from their lord before marrying. Others were subjected to the lord's legal system, which had no higher court for appeal. Serfs also needed approval if they wanted to transfer their land, however, they themselves could be transferred along with their land from one lord to another.

Hidden Meaning

Analyzing Key Concepts
Recommended Use: Guided Practice
EL

Hidden Meaning

Strategy and Activity

Write the word Inquisition on the board or use an overhead projector. Ask students to think about what this word means. Have them brainstorm words, events, and ideas that they associate with this word. Record these for everyone to see. Then explain that this word comes from the Latin word *inquisitio,* which is from the Latin verb inquirere, meaning "to inquire." When the word is capitalized, it refers specifically to the Catholic Church's court responsible for finding and dealing with Church heretics. Even though the last Inquisition, the Spanish Inquisition, ended in 1834, the term inquisition today is most often associated with these investigations that ignored human rights. During the Inquisitions, an accused was only given two options—confess or don't confess. Either way, the accused was found guilty. Ask students to think about ways they have heard the word *inquisition* used in everyday conversation. Did the person using the word mean to imply that the investigators were being unfair?

A New Age of Authors

Interdisciplinary Connection:
Language Arts Skill: Analyze Literature
Recommended Use: Team-Teaching
Strategy
AL

A New Age of Authors—An In-Depth Activity

Background

Female intellectuals found convents a haven for their activities. Most learned women of the Middle Ages, especially in Germany, were nuns. This was certainly true of Hildegard of Bingen, who became abbess of a religious house for females in western Germany. Hildegard was one of the first important women composers. She was an important contributor to the body of music known as Gregorian chant. Her work is especially remarkable because she succeeded at a time when music, especially sacred music, was almost exclusively the domain of men.

Strategy

Ask students to turn to page 800 in Glencoe Literature's *The Reader's Choice: World Literature* to read Bisclavret: *The Lay of the Werewolf* by Marie de France, translated by Robert Hanning and Joan Ferrante. Marie de France was possibly of noble birth, like Hildegard of Bingen. In Europe during the early Middle Ages, women were usually considered inferior to men. Because some women did write literature in the Middle Ages, historians have been provided with insight into the world of women during this time period. Marie lived sometime during the late twelfth century. Little is known of her life, but it is obvious that she was well educated. Some believe she may have been an abbess, like Hildegard. Marie often wrote about love saving someone trapped in a hostile world. Her style of writing is storytelling with rhyming couplets.

> He tore the nose off her face.
> What worse thing could he have done to her?
> Now men closed in on him from all sides;
> they were about to tear him apart,
> when a wise man said to the king,
> "My lord, listen to me!
> This beast has stayed with you,
> and there's not one of us
> who hasn't watched him closely,
> hasn't traveled with him often.

Inform students that they might find parts of the story grotesque.

Activities

Ask students the following questions, and then have them complete the activity below.

1. What prevents Bisclavret from turning into his human self? *(Without his clothes, Bisclavret would stay a werewolf forever.)*

2. How do you think the wife might be a metaphor for proper medieval society? *(Possible answer: The wife is not open to change. She does not accept her husband as a wild animal.)*

3. **Writing Prompt** Ask students to write about an incident when someone they know was unfairly punished. Encourage them to use poetry or metaphors.

CHAPTER 11

THE AMERICAS

Key Terms and Reinforcement
Strategy and Activity

Compile a list of key terms for this chapter. Include words such as:

longhouse	hieroglyph
clan	tribute
tepee	maize
adobe	*quipu*
pueblo	

Ask students to complete a word web. Demonstrate for students the structure of a word web that includes the following components:

- word history
- related words
- synonyms
- antonyms
- part of speech
- dictionary definition
- original sentence using the word
- how the word relates to the chapter

As students encounter the word in the text, they should add to their word webs the sentence from the text that uses the word. Supply college-level dictionaries, thesauri, and word-origin dictionaries. Provide a model of the word web, using an overhead projector.

Key Terms and Reinforcement
Independent Practice Skill: Use Word Webs to Analyze Important Terms
Recommended Use: Reinforcement
OL

Five Peoples Across America
Strategy and Activity

Instruct students to copy a map of North America either electronically or by hand. As students read Section 1, have them indicate on the map where each group of Native Americans lived and record the group's name in the center of that area. To extend this activity, have students write two or three facts for each Native American group under the group's name on the map.

Five Peoples Across America
Making a Map
Recommended Use:
Concept Reinforcement
BL

Learn More About
The Iroquois League

Have students use library or Internet sources to learn more about the Iroquois League and its member groups. Are any of the original groups still together? If so, how do they keep their culture alive? What more can you find out about Hiawatha and Deganawida, the instigators of the Great Peace?

Mayans, Aztecs, Incans
Strategy and Activity

Organize students into small groups. Have each group choose one of the civilizations from Mesoamerica or South America. Instruct them to prepare a presentation for the rest of the class. The presentations should be packed with images of the civilization's arts and culture. Allow time for a discussion after all the presentations. Discuss the differences between these three distinct cultures.

Mayans, Aztecs, Incans
Making a Presentation
Recommended Use: Enrichment
BL

Civilization Downfall
*Writing an Essay
Recommended Use:
Concept Introduction
AL*

Civilization Downfall
Strategy and Activity

The demise of each great civilization of Mesoamerica and South America through Spanish conquest was unique given the civilization's government, religion, and military. Each conquistador's method was different as well. Some conquistadors had large military forces, some were excellent tacticians, and some were just plain lucky. Ask students to write an essay that compares and contrasts how each civilization fell. Encourage students to use outside sources to enhance their essays.

People & Places
Alice Dixon Le Plongeon

Alice Dixon Le Plongeon was an amateur archaeologist and photographer who spent several years at the end of the nineteenth century with her husband, Augustus Le Plongeon, studying and photographing archaeological sites in the Yucatán and Central America. Even though their theories concerning the origins of the Maya culture were speculative and known to be false, their documentation of several Maya sites is considered an important contribution to American archaeology.

Mesoamerican Literature
*Interdisciplinary Connection:
Language Arts
Skill: Analyze Literature
Recommended Use: Team-Teaching
Strategy
AL*

Mesoamerican Literature—An In-Depth Activity
Background

Crucial to Mayan civilization was its belief that all of life was in the hands of divine powers. The name of their supreme god was Itzamna or "Lizard House." Gods were ranked in order of importance. Some, like the jaguar god of night, were evil rather than good. Like other ancient civilizations in Mesoamerica, the Maya practiced human sacrifice as a way to appease the gods. Human sacrifices were also used for special ceremonial occasions. When a male heir was presented to the throne, war captives were tortured and beheaded. In A.D. 790, one Mayan ruler took his troops into battle to gain prisoners for a celebration honoring his son.

Strategy

Ask students to turn to page 1040 in Glencoe Literature's *The Reader's Choice: World Literature* to read a hymn from the Popol Vuh, translated by Ralph Nelson. The Popul Vuh is considered a very important piece of Mesoamerican literature since it is one of the few sacred texts to survive. Missionaries destroyed most of the other Maya hieroglyphic books. The original version was written in Quiché, a Mayan language spoken in Guatemala. That version was lost, but a translation into Spanish by the Christian friar Francisco Ximénez did survive. Ask your students to think about what this creation myth means and how it sheds light on Mayan culture.

Before the world was created, Calm and Silence were the great kings that ruled. Nothing existed, there was nothing. Things had not yet been drawn together, the face of the earth was unseen. There was only motionless sea, and a great emptiness of sky. There were no men anywhere, or animals, no birds or fish, no crabs. Trees, stones, caves, grass, forests, none of these existed yet. There was nothing that could roar or run, nothing that could tremble or cry in the air. Flatness and emptiness, only the sea, alone and breathless. It was night; silence stood in the dark.

Activities

Ask students the following questions, and then have them complete the activity below.

1. How is this different from other creation stories you've read? Give examples. *(Answers may vary. Possible answers might include: In the Christian Bible, God makes man on the first attempt.)*

2. How do you think the wife might be a metaphor for proper medieval society? *(Possible answer: The wife is not open to change. She does not accept her husband as a wild animal.)*

3. **Writing Prompt** Ask students to work with a partner and research other Mesoamerican texts such as the Mayan and Aztec codices. Instruct them to write a brief paper or outline about what they've learned.

Key Terms and Reinforcement
Strategy and Activity

Compile a list of key terms for this chapter. Include words such as:

urban society	vernacular	Lutheranism
secular	fresco	predestination
mercenaries	Christian humanism	annul
dowry	salvation	
humanism	indulgences	

Ask students to complete a word web. Demonstrate for students the structure of a word web that includes the following components:

- word history
- related words
- synonyms
- antonyms
- part of speech
- dictionary definition
- original sentence using the word
- how the word relates to the chapter

As students encounter the word in the text, they should add to their word webs the sentence from the text that uses the word. Supply college-level dictionaries, thesauri, and word-origin dictionaries. Provide a model of the word web, using an overhead projector.

Renaissance Women
Strategy and Activity

Have students look up the term *Renaissance man*. Ask students if they can name some modern Renaissance men and women. Then explain that although the term probably was coined with men such as Leonardo da Vinci in mind, there were some very accomplished women who lived during the Renaissance period. Ask students to research and present oral presentations on a "Renaissance woman" who lived in fifteenth-to-seventeenth-century Europe. Some suggestions might be Isabella d'Este, Queen Elizabeth I of England, Catherine de Medici, Sofonisba Anguissola, and Artemesia Gentileschi.

Italian Art Renaissance
Strategy and Activity

Ask students to create a time line based on art in the Italian Renaissance. It should include birth and death dates as well as the completion date of one major piece of work for the following artists: Leonardo da Vinci, Niccolò Machiavelli, Michelangelo, Raphael. A Web site to check out is Timeline of Art History at www.metmuseum.org/toah/ht/08/eusts/ht08eusts.htm from the Metropolitan Museum of Art.

Humanism Versus Humanism
Comparing Key Concepts
Recommended Use:
Classroom Discussion
OL

Humanism Versus Humanism

Strategy and Activity

Encourage students to participate in a discussion comparing humanism and Christian humanism. What was the goal of humanism? What was the goal of Christian humanism? How are these goals similar, and how do they relate to the works of Petrarch and Desiderius Erasmus? How did the idea of returning to the foundations affect culture and religion? At the end of this discussion, ask students to write a brief paragraph about humanism and Christian humanism based on the class discussion.

People & Places
Leonardo da Vinci

Besides being an artist, Leonardo da Vinci had many other achievements. Have students research Leonardo's work in a field other than art and prepare a report or poster detailing his contributions in that area.

The Drama of the Renaissance
Writing a Dramatic Scene
Recommended Use: Chapter Wrap-Up
OL

The Drama of the Renaissance

Strategy and Activity

Have students break into groups of four or more. Instruct each group to write a dramatic scene based on the information in the text about Piero di Lorenzo de' Medici and Girolamo Savonarola. Inform them that the Medici family patronized Girolamo Savonarola. At that time, a corrupt pope, Alexander VI, tried to bribe the powerful Savonarola. When that did not work and once Savonarola's popularity waned, Pope Alexander VI had him excommunicated and executed. Encourage students to be creative, and tell them that they are allowed some artistic license. Plan class time so groups can act out their written scenes.

Humanist Love
Interdisciplinary Connection:
Language Arts
Skill: Analyze Literature
Recommended Use:
Independent Practice
AL

Humanist Love—An In-Depth Activity

Background

Petrarch, who has often been called the father of Italian Renaissance humanism, did more than any other individual in the fourteenth century to foster the development of humanism. Petrarch looked for forgotten Latin manuscripts and set in motion a search for similar manuscripts in monastic libraries throughout Europe. He also began the humanist emphasis on using pure classical Latin (Latin as used by the ancient Romans as opposed to medieval Latin). Humanists used the works of Cicero as a model for prose and those of Virgil for poetry.

Strategy

Ask students to turn to page 846 in Glencoe Literature's *The Reader's Choice: World Literature* to read "Laura" from *Canzoniere* by Petrarch, translated by Morris Bishop. Francesco Petrarca, known in English as Petrarch, wrote an entire collection of love sonnets with a woman named Laura as the focus. Petrarch's love for Laura is unrequited. The *Canzoniere* is thought to cover a 40-year period that spans the life and death of Laura.

> She seemed divine among the dreary folk
> Of earth. You say she is not so today?
> Well, though the bow's unbent, the wound bleeds on.

Even though little is known about Laura's true identity in history, it is certain she was the cause of much joy and pain in Petrarch's love sonnets.

Activities

Ask students the following questions, and then have them complete the activity below.

1. Find two similes and/or metaphors in the selection from *Canzoniere*. *(Possible answers: She seemed divine, love's tinder heaped upon my breast.)*

2. Read "Sonnet 239" on page 853 of Glencoe Literature's *The Reader's Choice: World Literature*. How is Michelangelo's sonnet similar and yet different than Petrach's sonnet? *("Laura" and "Sonnet 239" are both about love. The love in "Laura" seems unattainable, whereas the love in "Sonnet 239" is part of the author's life.)*

3. **Writing Prompt** Ask students to research Giovanni Boccaccio, who was a friend of Petrarch's. Ask them to write a brief paper comparing the lives and works of the two authors.

CHAPTER 13 — THE AGE OF EXPLORATION

Key Terms and Reinforcement

Strategy and Activity

Compile a list of key terms for this chapter. Include words such as:

conquistadors	balance of trade	*peninsulares*
encomienda	subsidies	creoles
Columbian Exchange	plantations	mulattoes
colony	triangular trade	*mita*
mercantilism	Middle Passage	

Ask students to complete a word web. Demonstrate for students the structure of a word web that includes the following components:

- word history
- related words
- synonyms
- antonyms
- part of speech
- dictionary definition
- original sentence using the word
- how the word relates to the chapter

As students encounter the word in the text, they should add to their word webs the sentence from the text that uses the word. Supply college-level dictionaries, thesauri, and word-origin dictionaries. Provide a model of the word web, using an overhead projector.

Adventure and Destruction

Strategy and Activity

Help students organize into small groups. Tell them that they will be writing a skit or song about their chosen topic. Have each group pick a topic from the following list: Portuguese explorers, Spanish explorers, Spanish Empire, European rivals. Make sure that each topic gets chosen by at least one group. Instruct students to use information and details from the section text to help them create something both entertaining and informative. Encourage groups to either read or perform what they wrote.

Learn More About
Colonial Living

In 2004 PBS aired a television series called *Colonial House*. The program showed people trying to live as the English colonists did at Plymouth in 1628. The participants had to leave the modern world, including their homes, jobs, and friends, to live as a community with strangers. They also had to live by the laws and wear the clothing of Plymouth colonists. The colony was agricultural, so the participants in this show had to work the land and use the harvest as their primary food source. The show presented an interesting look into the challenges faced by colonists in the New World.

Key Terms and Reinforcement
Independent Practice Skill: Use Word Webs to Analyze Important Terms
Recommended Use: Reinforcement
OL

Adventure and Destruction
Performing a Skit or Song
Recommended Use: Section Wrap-Up
BL

Copyright © Glencoe/McGraw-Hill, a division of The McGraw-Hill Companies, Inc.

Inca Who?
Making Predictions
Recommended Use:
Writing Assignment
OL

Inca Who?
Strategy and Activity

Have students write an essay from the viewpoint of a Spanish soldier meeting the Incans with Pizarro in 1532. Tell them that their essay should contain predictions about what will become of the great Inca Empire. Have them base their predictions on facts about the empire. Remind them that the Inca Empire had a system of roads extending in all directions that totaled 24,800 miles. One road even went through the Andes. The Inca Empire probably consisted of 12 million people at the time of Pizarro's attack, extending over 2,100 miles along South America's western coast. There were buildings and monuments made to withstand earthquakes and irrigation systems for crops. The society was very organized and enjoyed cultural activities such as theatrical plays.

Slavery
Analyzing Key Concepts
Recommended Use:
Cross Curriculum—Economics
AL

Slavery
Strategy and Activity

The slave trade increased in the New World due to the desired production of sugarcane. The Spanish wanted to produce more and more sugarcane in the West Indies, but the work was very labor-intensive. The people living in the West Indies could not do all the work. What do students think the role of slavery in economics has been throughout history and, in particular, during European expansion? Ask students if they think slavery is still a part of the workforce in some countries and if it will always exist somewhere.

New World
Interdisciplinary Connection:
Language Arts
Skill: Analyze Literature
Recommended Use: Team-Teaching
Strategy
AL

New World—An In-Depth Activity
Strategy

Convinced that Earth's circumference was not as great as others thought, Christopher Columbus believed he could reach Asia by sailing west instead of east around Africa. Columbus persuaded Queen Isabella of Spain to finance an exploratory expedition. In October 1492, he reached the Americas and explored the coastline of Cuba and the island of Hispaniola. Government-sponsored explorers from many countries joined the race to the Americas. A Venetian seaman, John Cabot, explored the New England coastline of the Americas for England. The Portuguese sea captain Pedro Cabral landed in South America in 1500. Amerigo Vespucci, a Florentine, went along on several voyages. Vespucci's letters describing the voyages led to the use of the name America (after Amerigo) for the new lands. Europeans called these territories the New World. However, they already had flourishing civilizations made up of millions of people when the Europeans arrived. The Americas were, of course, new to the Europeans, who quickly saw opportunities for conquest and exploitation.

Strategy

Ask students to turn to page 1067 in Glencoe Literature's *The Reader's Choice: World Literature* to read "Discoveries" by Eduardo Langagne. The author was born in Mexico City in 1952. Langagne is an award-winning writer who has also translated many Bulgarian poems. In his poem "Discoveries," he alludes to people, places, and events that are related to the European explorations of the New World. He mentions caravels, which were the vessels in which Spanish and Portuguese sailors traveled. Christopher Columbus had traveled to the Americas in caravels for some of his voyages. Langagne also alludes to Amerigo Vespucci. He compares the Americas to a woman and implies that Columbus did not discover her nor did Vespucci map her.

columbus did not discover this woman
nor do her eyes resemble caravels
vespucci never mapped her hair

Vespucci did travel to the Americas several times. He even ventured to the mouth of the Amazon River and reached the coast of Brazil and possibly made it to the Rio de la Plata. Based on these voyages, it became obvious that the Americas were not part of Asia. In 1507 a German mapmaker suggested that these new lands be named after Amerigo Vespucci. Have volunteers take turns reading aloud this poem. Ask students to close their eyes while they listen and try to see the imagery the author is creating.

Activities

Ask students the following questions, and then have them complete the activity below.

1. How is the woman in the poem similar to the Americas? How is this metaphor extended throughout the poem? *(She was in the west, she was unknown, and she took a long time to find. The metaphor is extended throughout because almost every line compares the woman and the Americas.)*

2. Why do you think the author implies that Columbus did not discover the Americas? *(Possible answer: because the Americas already had people living there when Columbus arrived. In addition, Columbus was is search of a route to Asia not new territory for Spain.)*

3. **Writing Prompt** Ask students to write an essay giving their opinion about the fact that Columbus has been credited with the "discovery" of the Americas.

CHAPTER 14 CRISIS AND ABSOLUTISM IN EUROPE

Key Terms and Reinforcement

Strategy and Activity

Compile a list of key terms for this chapter. Include words such as:

militant	divine right of kings	czar
armada	commonwealth	Mannerism
inflation	absolutism	natural rights
witchcraft	boyars	baroque

Ask students to complete a word web. Demonstrate for students the structure of a word web that includes the following components:

- word history
- related words
- synonyms
- antonyms
- part of speech
- dictionary definition
- original sentence using the word
- how the word relates to the chapter

As students encounter the word in the text, they should add to their word webs the sentence from the text that uses the word. Supply college-level dictionaries, thesauri, and word-origin dictionaries. Provide a model of the word web, using an overhead projector.

Spanish Words

Strategy and Activity

Point out the vocabulary term *armada*. The term is Spanish and comes from the Latin *armata*. It means "a fleet of warships." Draw two columns on the board. Label one "Word" and the other "Meaning." Have students brainstorm a list of Spanish words that are used in the English language. Record those in the first column. Then ask volunteers to provide the meanings for the words. You can begin with the word *armada* as an example. Discuss any words whose meaning is different when used in Spanish or English.

The End of Wars

Strategy and Activity

Religion was only part of the reason for the Thirty Years' War. Initially, Catholics and Protestants started the conflict in 1618. Eventually, most European nations became involved for political reasons. When the war ended in 1648, European borders were redrawn. The Thirty Years' War has been called the "last of the religious wars." There has not been a religious war since that involved so many different European nations. However, there have been wars about religion. Ask students to research conflicts in the twentieth and twenty-first centuries. Have them write a report on one that involved religion. Tell them to include the issues concerning both groups of people. Ask students to present their research to the entire class.

Sidebar notes

Key Terms and Reinforcement
Independent Practice Skill: Use Word Webs to Analyze Important Terms
Recommended Use: Reinforcement
OL

Spanish Words
Analyzing Words
Recommended Use: Enrichment
EL

The End of Wars
Understanding Key Concepts
Recommended Use: Research
AL

Political Thought

Comparing Political Theories
Recommended Use:
Cross-Curriculum—Political Science
OL

Political Thought
Strategy and Activity

Have students compare the political theories of Thomas Hobbes and John Locke. What role did each man think society and government should have? Whose theory is similar to the ideas stated in the American Declaration of Independence? Have students answer the previous question on a sheet of paper, providing facts about Hobbes's or Locke's beliefs that support their answer.

Don Quixote

Interdisciplinary Connection:
Language Arts Skill:
Analyze Literature
Recommended Use:
Team-Teaching Strategy
AL

Don Quixote—An In-Depth Activity
Background

One of the crowning achievements of the golden age of Spanish literature was the work of Miguel de Cervantes. His novel *Don Quixote* has been hailed as one of the greatest literary works of all time. In the two main characters of this famous work, Cervantes presented the dual nature of the Spanish character. The knight, Don Quixote from La Mancha, is the visionary so involved in his lofty ideals that he does not see the hard realities around him. To him, for example, windmills appear to be four-armed giants. In contrast, the knight's earthy squire, Sancho Panza, is a realist. Each of these characters finally comes to see the value of the other's perspective. The readers of *Don Quixote* are left with the conviction that both visionary dreams and the hard work of reality are necessary to the human condition.

Strategy

Ask students to turn to page 836 in Glencoe Literature's *The Reader's Choice: World Literature* to read an excerpt from *Don Quixote* by Miguel de Cervantes, translated by J. M. Cohen. Cohen translated this piece of literature in 1950. His translation is still one of the most read English translations. Invite students who know Spanish to read an excerpt of *Don Quixote* in its original language. Explain that the job of a translator is very challenging. Literal translations usually do not convey the meaning intended by the author. A translator has to be aware of what words and phrases meant at the time a work was written. Ask volunteers to translate the following line from *Don Quixote*: "Que trata de la condición y ejercicio del famoso hidalgo don Quijote de la Mancha." Have them leave any word that they cannot translate in its original Spanish. Then have students compare it to the translated first line by J. M. Cohen. *Don Quixote* has been translated into more than 60 languages. Some of these translations are also shortened versions of the original text.

> In a certain village in La Mancha, which I do not wish to name, there lived not long ago a gentleman—one of those who have always a lance in the rack, an ancient shield, a lean hack and a greyhound for coursing. His habitual diet consisted of a stew, more beef than mutton, of hash most nights, boiled bones on Saturdays, lentils on Fridays, and a young pigeon as a Sunday treat.

Activities

Ask students the following questions, and then have them complete the activity below.

1. Why do Don Quixote and Sancho Panza make a good team? *(Their individual traits balance each other.)*

2. What word, sentence, or part of the story does not make sense to you? You may want to exchange this query with a partner's query and work together to find answers. *(Answers will vary.)*

3. **Writing Prompt** Cervantes's novel had immediate success upon its release in 1605. Until this point in his life, Cervantes had been relatively poor. He was 58 years old the year Don Quixote was published. Have students write an essay about the possible effects of sudden fame.

CHAPTER 15

THE MUSLIM EMPIRES

Key Terms and Reinforcement
Strategy and Activity

Compile a list of key terms for this chapter. Include words such as:

janissaries	harem	orthodoxy
pashas	grand vizier	anarchy
gunpowder	ulema	zamindars
sultan	shah	suttee

Ask students to complete a word web. Demonstrate for students the structure of a word web that includes the following components:

- word history
- related words
- synonyms
- antonyms
- part of speech
- dictionary definition
- original sentence using the word
- how the word relates to the chapter

As students encounter the word in the text, they should add to their word webs the sentence from the text that uses the word. Supply college-level dictionaries, thesauri, and word-origin dictionaries. Provide a model of the word web, using an overhead projector.

Key Terms and Reinforcement
Independent Practice Skill: Use Word Webs to Analyze Important Terms Recommended Use: Reinforcement OL

The Islamic and European Worlds (1500–1800)

Ask students to create a time line showing political and cultural events in Europe and in the Islamic world between 1500 and 1800. European entries should be a different color than the Islamic items. Have students compare the two cultures and speculate on which events connected the two societies and which were completely independent. They should also consider how these events affected the common people of the time.

The Islamic and European Worlds (1500–1800)
*Creating a Time Line
Recommended Use: Chapter Opener
BL*

The Persian Monarchy
Strategy and Activity

The Safavid Dynasty was responsible for uniting all of present-day Iran under a Persian king. It also declared the official religion to be Shia, thus separating Iran from its neighbor. It also reached a level of success never reached before in Iran's post-Islamic history. Help students organize into groups. Tell them to research the five different dynasties that have ruled Iran and at least two significant facts about each dynasty. Once they have finished, lead a discussion that ends with the current Shia-influenced government.

The Persian Monarchy
*Conducting Research
Recommended Use: Group Practice
BL*

What If Vienna Had Fallen?

Have students suppose that Vienna had fallen to the Ottoman armies in 1529. Use a map of Europe in the sixteenth century to consider the next likely Ottoman moves into Europe. What resistance would they have met? What territory do students feel the Ottomans could have conquered and held? Let students discuss how 200 years of Ottoman rule over central Europe would have changed European culture.

What If Vienna Had Fallen?
*Class Discussion
Recommended Use: Chapter Wrap-Up
Level:BL*

Learn More About . . .
Janissaries

Have students use library or Internet sources to find out more about the janissaries in the Ottoman Empire and how Sultan Mahmud II eventually destroyed them during the Auspicious Incident.

The Empire Chart
Creating a Chart
Recommended Use: Chapter Wrap-Up
AL

The Empire Chart
Strategy and Activity

Have students review the chapter by outlining all three sections. Tell them they should pay special attention to the different Muslim empires and that they should record dates and at least two facts per empire or ruler. Instruct students to create a chart that contains all the empires and rulers mentioned in the chapter. They can organize the chart any way they want. It should contain the names of the empire, dates of their existence, and significant facts and rulers.

People & Places
Shah Abbas

Review with students the reasons that Shah Abbas was given the title "the Great." Ask if there is a ruler in the world today, or one that they have read about in the textbook, that has the same characteristics. Students should explain their answers.

Sultanate
Interdisciplinary Connection:
Language Arts
Skill: Analyze Literature
Recommended Use: Team-Teaching
Strategy
AL

Sultanate—An In-Depth Activity
Background

As the empire expanded, the status and prestige of the sultan increased. The position took on the trappings of imperial rule. A centralized administrative system was adopted, and the sultan became increasingly isolated from his people. The private domain of the sultan was called the harem ("sacred place"). Here, the sultan and his wives resided. Often a sultan chose four wives as his favorites.

Strategy

Ask students to turn to page 452 in Glencoe Literature's *The Reader's Choice: World Literature* to read from *The Thousand and One Nights,* translated by N. J. Dawood. The folklore and legends contained in *The Thousand and One Nights* were probably told for centuries before being written down. The collection contains an arching story line about a sultan who condemns his wife to death. The night before her death, she tells a very compelling story but ends it on a cliffhanger. The sultan must reprieve her death sentence for one more night so that she may finish her story.

From far and near men came to hear me speak of my adventures and to learn the news of foreign lands from me. All were astounded at the dangers I had escaped and wished me joy of my return. Such was my second voyage.

Tomorrow, my friends, if Allah wills, I shall relate to you the extraordinary tale of my third voyage.

She continues this storytelling process for 1,001 until the sultan lifts her sentence. The most popular stories from the collection are about Aladdin, Sindbad the sailor, and Ali Baba.

Activities

   Ask students the following questions, and then have them complete the activity that below.

1. Why does Sindbad leave Baghdad? *(He has a longing to travel and visit distant lands for profit and adventure.)*

2. Who do you suppose Sindbad the Porter is? *(He is the person whom Sindbad the Sailor tells his stories to. He is obviously not rich or a noble.)*

3. **Writing Prompt** Have students form small groups. Ask each group to write an eighth voyage. Arrange for your students to perform their drama in front of the class.

CHAPTER 16

THE EAST ASIAN WORLD

Key Terms and Reinforcement
Strategy and Activity

Compile a list of key terms for this chapter. Include words such as:

queue	porcelain	*eta*
banners	daimyo	bureaucracy
commercial capitalism	hans	mainland states
clan	hostage system	

Ask students to complete a word web. Demonstrate for students the structure of a word web that includes the following components:

- word history
- related words
- synonyms
- antonyms
- part of speech
- dictionary definition
- original sentence using the word
- how the word relates to the chapter

As students encounter the word in the text, they should add to their word webs the sentence from the text that uses the word. Supply college-level dictionaries, thesauri, and word-origin dictionaries. Provide a model of the word web, using an overhead projector.

The Hermit Kingdom
Strategy and Activity

Ask students to consider the idea of isolationism. What are the advantages? What are the disadvantages? Discuss the policies of isolationism in the Yi dynasty. How do they compare with modern day North Korea? Have the class research the history of North Korea, specifically in regards to its policy of self-reliance. Instruct them to write a brief comparison of North Korea and the Yi dynasty. If time permits, continue the discussion and encourage students to share what they have learned through research.

People & Places
The *Eta*

The *etas* were the outcasts of Japanese feudal society. Laws were enacted to regulate their clothes, place of habitation, and hairstyle. In modern Japan, they are a minority and are referred to as the *burakumin*, because *eta* is considered a derogatory term. Have students use library or Internet sources to find out more about the *eta*, their history, and where they fit into modern Japanese society.

Key Terms and Reinforcement
Independent Practice Skill: Use Word Webs to Analyze Important Terms
Recommended Use: Reinforcement
OL

The Hermit Kingdom
Identifying Central Issues
Recommended Use: Class Discussion
OL

An Alternate History
Strategy and Activity

The voyages of Zheng He were a fascinating part of Chinese history. The exchange of goods and culture left its mark on China. What might have happened if China had made it to other parts of the world before Europe did? Start a discussion about how history might have been different if China developed as an imperialistic power before Europe. Instruct students to consider this "alternate history" while they read the chapter. After students have completed the chapter, revisit the idea of the alternate history. Mention Spain's influence on Central and South America and the influx of gold and silver into Europe. In addition, ask students how the history of North America would have changed. Would there be countries similar to the United States, Mexico, and Canada?

Edo Culture
Interdisciplinary Connection:
Language Arts
Skill: Analyze Literature
Recommended Use:
Team-Teaching Strategy
AL

Edo Culture—An In-Depth Activity
Background

A major economic change took place under the Tokugawa. Since the fourteenth century, many upper-class Japanese, influenced by Confucianism, had considered trade and industry beneath them. Under the Tokugawa rulers, however, trade and industry began to flourish as never before, especially in the growing cities of Edo, (now Tokyo) Kyōto, and Ōsaka. By 1750 Edo had a population of over a million and was one of the largest cities in the world. Banking flourished, and paper money became the normal medium of exchange in business transactions. A Japanese merchant class emerged and began to play a significant role in the life of the Japanese nation.

Strategy

Ask students to turn to page 640 in Glencoe Literature's *The Reader's Choice: World Literature* to read the haiku by Yosa Buson, translated by Geoffrey Bownas and Anthony Thwaite. Buson was born in 1716 and studied painting and poetry in Edo. He is considered the haiku's second-greatest master after Matsuo Bashō. During the Tokugawa Era (1603–1868), popular literature and the arts began to flourish. Buson's interest in painting is evident in his poetry.

Spring rain:	Spring rain:
Telling a tale as they go,	Soaking on the roof
Straw cape, umbrella.	A child's rag ball.

Remind students that the haiku is a Japanese poetry form consisting of very few words. Ask volunteers to read aloud from page 641. Explain that many of the words are chosen for what they suggest. Encourage students to think about each word they hear.

Activities

Ask students the following questions, and then have them complete the activity below.

1. What do you like most about Buson's poetry? *(Answers will vary.)*

2. What is happening in both poems? *(It is raining.)*

3. **Writing Prompt** Ask students to write a haiku about their favorite season. Tell them that the poem should have three lines, the first with five syllables, the second with seven syllables, and the last with five syllables.

CHAPTER 17

REVOLUTION AND ENLIGHTENMENT

Key Terms and Reinforcement
Strategy and Activity

Compile a list of key terms for this chapter. Include words such as:

scientific method	social contract
philosophe	enlightened absolutism
deism	federal system

Ask students to complete a word web. Demonstrate for students the structure of a word web that includes the following components:

- word history
- related words
- synonyms
- antonyms
- part of speech
- dictionary definition
- original sentence using the word
- how the word relates to the chapter

As students encounter the word in the text, they should add to their word webs the sentence from the text that uses the word. Supply college-level dictionaries, thesauri, and word-origin dictionaries. Provide a model of the word web, using an overhead projector.

Patriot or Loyalist?
Strategy and Activity

When the American Revolution began, not all of the colonists supported the fight for independence. Have students consider the benefits and disadvantages of America becoming an independent nation. Organize the class into groups, with half of each group's members assuming the role of Revolutionaries, or Patriots, and the other half playing Loyalists, supporters of the British Crown. Have each group present an informed debate on the issues, political and economic. What were the disadvantages of starting a war with Britain? What benefits did the American colonists hope to achieve with their fight for independence?

People & Places
Catherine the Great

Have students use library and Internet sources to research the descendants of Catherine II and the succession of Russian monarchs. Then have students create a family tree for Catherine II so that they understand how many Russian rulers were her descendants. Discuss with students the relationship of each predecessor and successor from Peter III to Nicholas II.

Key Terms and Reinforcement
Independent Practice Skill: Use Word Webs to Analyze Important Terms
Recommended Use: Reinforcement
OL

Patriot or Loyalist?
Stage a Debate
Recommended Use: Guided Practice
OL

Leaders of the Scientific Revolution
Create a Chart
Recommended Use:
Chapter Wrap-Up
OL

Leaders of the "Scientific" Revolution
Strategy and Activity

As students read through the first section of the chapter "Revolution and Enlightenment," have them list the major contributions of Isaac Newton, Maria Winkelmann, and Francis Bacon. Then ask students to complete a chart identifying other men and women who contributed to the Scientific Revolution between the sixteenth and eighteenth centuries. Students should write each person's field of study and most important accomplishments. Afterwards, have students discuss the significance of these discoveries and ideas. How did they help to determine what "science" is? Why were they so revolutionary at the time they were first recognized?

New Developments in Music
Classroom Demonstration
Recommended Use:
Enrichment
AL

New Developments in Music
Strategy and Activity

Play for students a variety of music from the eighteenth century, including Bach, Handel, Haydn, and Mozart. Try to find pieces that students might be familiar with, such as Handel's *Hallelujah Chorus,* Haydn's *Surprise Symphony,* Bach's *Brandenburg Concerto,* or Mozart's piano variations on *Twinkle, Twinkle, Little Star.* They might be surprised that they recognize some "classical" music. Discuss some of the characteristics of Baroque and classical music and how the compositions you have chosen are examples of this musical period.

Is Rousseau Right?
Evaluate an Argument
Recommended Use:
Classroom Discussion
BL

Is Rousseau Right?
Strategy and Activity

Ask students to reread the section on Jean-Jacques Rousseau in their textbooks and do additional research on his *Discourse on the Origins of the Inequality of Mankind.* Have students evaluate Rousseau's argument that governments and laws are made to protect private property but in fact enslave the people who created them. Do students feel their government protects or endangers their property? Do they feel served or enslaved by government? What reasonable alternatives do students see to having a strong central government? How might Rousseau's ideas have contributed to the creation of socialist or anarchist ideas in the nineteenth century?

Communication and Politics
Make Inferences and
Draw Conclusions
Recommended Use:
Classroom Discussion
OL

Communication and Politics
Strategy and Activity

Between the sixteenth and eighteenth centuries, transatlantic travel was slow and uncertain. It often took more than 60 days to get an answer from Spain, France, or England to a question posed by a local governor in the Americas. Discuss with the class the effect of slow communication on the politics of European countries and their colonies.

Differentiated Instruction for the World History Classroom

European Feminism—An In-Depth Activity

Background

For centuries, male intellectuals had argued that the nature of women made them inferior to men and made male domination of women necessary. By the eighteenth century, however, female thinkers began to express their ideas about improving the condition of women. Mary Wollstonecraft, the English writer, advanced the strongest statement for the rights of women. Many see her as the founder of the modern European and American movement for women's rights. In *A Vindication of the Rights of Women,* Wollstonecraft identified two problems with the views of many Enlightenment thinkers. She noted that the same people who argued that women must obey men also said that government based on the arbitrary power of monarchs over their subjects was wrong. Wollstonecraft pointed out that the power of men over women was equally wrong. Wollstonecraft further argued that the Enlightenment was based on an ideal of reason in all human beings. Because women have reason, they are entitled to the same rights as men.

Strategy

Ask students to turn to page 850 in Glencoe Literature's *The Reader's Choice: World Literature* to read "Sonnet 8" by Louise Labé, translated by Willis Barnstone. Point out that although many may see Wollstonecraft as the founder of the movement for women's rights, Labé is touted as Wollstonecraft's feminist predecessor. Petrarchan love sonnets are typically written from the male perspective, and the male is usually speaking to a woman whom he loves, but who is aloof and inaccessible. This sonnet is written in the Petrarchan tradition, but Labé provides her own feminist perspective by writing her love poetry from the woman's point of view:

> So Love inconstantly leads me in vain and when I think my sorrow has no end unthinkingly I find I have no pain. But when it seems that joy is in my reign

> And an ecstatic hour is mine to spend, He comes and I, in ancient grief, descend.

Obviously, Labé's poetry was confusing to readers who were accustomed to unrealistic descriptions of the emotions of love. She addressed her poetry to knowledgeable readers who could appreciate the positions she was taking in relation to the conventions of her time.

Activities

Ask students the following questions, and then have them complete the activity below.

1. What is suggested about love in this poem? *(Love creates a mixture of emotions in people, and often these emotions seem to conflict.)*

2. How does the poet create the conflicting imagery of love? *(Labé creates a series of oxymorons, such as "extremely hot in suffering cold" and "in my pleasure I endure deep grief.")*

3. **Writing Prompt** Ask students to research the topic of feminism in America as well as in other major countries. After educating themselves about the positions and arguments on both sides of the issue, ask students to construct a position paper arguing for or against complete equal rights for women.

European Feminism
Interdisciplinary Connection: Language Arts
Skill: Analyze Literature
Recommended Use: Team-Teaching Strategy
AL

CHAPTER 18

THE FRENCH REVOLUTION AND NAPOLEON

Key Terms and Reinforcement

Strategy and Activity

Compile a list of key terms for this chapter. Include words such as:

estate	coup d'état
bourgeoisie	consulate
faction	nationalism
elector	

Ask students to complete a word web. Demonstrate for students the structure of a word web that includes the following components:

- word history
- related words
- synonyms
- antonyms
- part of speech
- dictionary definition
- original sentence using the word
- how the word relates to the chapter

As students encounter the word in the text, they should add to their word webs the sentence from the text that uses the word. Supply college-level dictionaries, thesauri, and word-origin dictionaries. Provide a model of the word web, using an overhead projector.

Support or Oppose the Revolution

Strategy and Activity

Organize students into groups and assign each group a particular stage of the French Revolution or Napoleon's reign. Have group members write two editorials. The first should explain why they support a particular political group or movement from their assigned time period. The second will state the opposite opinion, explaining why they oppose the group or movement. The editorial must use facts and examples to support its argument.

Declaration of the Rights of Young Adults and the Student

Strategy and Activity

The Declaration of the Rights of Man and the Citizen declared the freedom and liberties pursued by the French people. The Declaration of the Rights of Woman and the Female Citizen proclaimed the equality of rights that women were entitled to. Have students write their own Declaration of the Rights of Young Adults and Students. In it, they will present the 10 rights that they believe are basic to all students. Afterwards, compare answers and decide with the class which 10 rights should be used for a final declaration. The class should then write a conclusion that states the benefits they believe will result from the adoption of the declaration. The final document should be made into a poster and displayed in the classroom.

The French Revolution
Create a Chart
Recommended Use:
Chapter Wrap-Up
BL

The French Revolution
Strategy and Activity

The French Revolution did more than simply replace one government with another. It involved a whole series of changes in government and social institutions as French society remade itself. Have students form groups to create a two-column chart showing the stages of the revolution. They should list each stage or event and its dates in one column. The second column should describe the stage or event, including documents and important leaders. The first two stages should be the Old Regime and the meeting of the Estates-General. Have students compare their charts.

People & Places
Les Miserables

Victor Hugo's novel *Les Miserables* depicts life in early nineteenth-century France. Show a video of the film in class or have students read the book. Then discuss which parts of Hugo's story are historically realistic and which are imaginative and fictionalized. How are the various people and classes portrayed?

Napoleon Bonaparte
Synthesize Information
Recommended Use:
Chapter Wrap-Up
EL

Napoleon Bonaparte
Strategy and Activity

Although Napoleon's achievements were many, historians differ about his place in history. Organize students into groups and ask them to evaluate Napoleon's career. They should make a list with the following headings: Military Leader, Political Ruler, Social Reformer, Empire Builder. Then under each heading, they should list Napoleon's actions and contributions, using information from the textbook and additional resources if necessary. After compiling the lists, students should discuss whether Napoleon was a force for good or ill, and whether he helped advance human society or hindered progress.

Internet Learning
Napoleon's Battles

Students can get a feel for what Napoleon's battles were like by going to www.pbs.org/empires/napoleon. This Web site offers an interactive battlefield simulator, where students can reenact the Battle of Waterloo. There are also interesting descriptions of Napoleon's campaigns and the lives of his soldiers.

Napoleon Bonaparte—An In-Depth Activity

Background

Napoleon Bonaparte dominated French and European history from 1799 to 1815. As a young man, Napoleon won a scholarship to a famous military school. When he completed his studies, Napoleon was commissioned as a lieutenant in the French army. Although he became one of the world's greatest generals and a man beloved by his soldiers, there were few signs of his future success at this stage. He spoke with an Italian accent and was not popular with his fellow officers. Napoleon devoted himself to his goals. He read what French philosophers had to say about reason, and he studied famous military campaigns. Napoleon rose quickly through the ranks. Napoleon won a series of battles with qualities he became famous for—speed, surprise, and decisive action. His keen intelligence, ease with words, and supreme self-confidence allowed him to win the support of those around him. Napoleon's downfall began in 1812 when he decided to invade Russia. Within only a few years, his fall was complete. In 1821 Napoleon died while in exile, but his memory haunted French political life for many decades.

Strategy

Ask students to turn to page 873 in Glencoe Literature's *The Reader's Choice: World Literature* to read *Russia 1812* by Victor Hugo, translated by Robert Lowell. Explain to students that this is an excerpt from Victor Hugo's poem *The Expiation* in which he shows how Napoleon's political crime of seizing power illegally was paid for, or expiated, by his eventual downfall. When Napoleon led his army to Russia in 1812, he expected a quick battle. Czar Alexander I, however, chose a strategy of retreat and drew the French army deep into Moscow. When Napoleon entered Moscow, the Russians had set fire to the city and abandoned it, forcing the French to retreat. As the army attempted to make its way back to France, the bitter winter and the czar's army proved to be formidable enemies. "For the first time the 'Eagle' [Napoleon] bowed his head," for he had required his troops to swear by the standard that they would conquer or die. Napoleon seemed to know the direction he and his troops were headed, as beaten, dying, and attacked constantly by the cold and the Russians, the emperor "felt terrified":

> "God of armies, is this the end?" he cried. And then at last the expiation came, as he heard someone who called him by his name. . . . Napoleon understood, restless, bareheaded, leaden, as he stood before his butchered legions in the snow.

Activities

Ask students the following questions, and then have them complete the activity below.

1. What two forces worked against Napoleon? What characteristics defined these forces? *(The two forces were the extreme cold and the Russian czar's army. Both were formidable and relentless.)*

2. What does Napoleon understand at the end of this poem? *(that his reign was over; that he was beaten)*

3. **Writing Prompt** Organize the students into groups and assign each group a different portion of Napoleon Bonaparte's life. Ask each group to use its research to write a mock interview with the emperor, and then to present the interview to the rest of the class. Close by asking students to use the information from the interviews to summarize how they would have responded to Bonaparte.

Napoleon Bonaparte
Interdisciplinary Connection:
Language Arts
Skill: Analyze Literature
Recommended Use:
Team-Teaching Strategy
AL

INDUSTRIALIZATION AND NATIONALISM

Key Terms and Reinforcement
Strategy and Activity
Compile a list of key terms for this chapter. Include words such as:

capital	liberalism
entrepreneurs	militarism
cottage industry	emancipation
socialism	secede
conservatism	realism

Ask students to complete a word web. Demonstrate for students the structure of a word web that includes the following components:

- word history
- related words
- synonyms
- antonyms
- part of speech
- dictionary definition
- original sentence using the word
- how the word relates to the chapter

As students encounter the word in the text, they should add to their word webs the sentence from the text that uses the word. Supply college-level dictionaries, thesauri, and word-origin dictionaries. Provide a model of the word web, using an overhead projector.

Key Terms and Reinforcement
Independent Practice Skill: Use Word Webs to Analyze Important Terms
Recommended Use: Reinforcement
OL

Division of Labor
Strategy and Activity
To help your students understand the concepts of division of labor and mass production, organize the class into groups of 10 to work together to complete a particular task. It can be as simple as a drawing, or the task might involve a more complicated assembly. Five students in each group will perform the entire task as individuals; the others will divide the work. For example, with a drawing of a person, have each of five students complete the entire task individually, while the other five choose a particular part (arm, legs, face, torso) to draw and then pass the drawing on to the next person. All drawings can be timed and judged for quality. Discuss the results as a class. In which way was the task finished most quickly? Who had the greatest satisfaction? The best product? Speculate about the types of tasks that best lend themselves to division of labor and which types are most efficiently done individually. *(assembly of a car versus production of a work of art; packaging of tuna versus open-heart surgery)*

Division of Labor
Create an Assembly Line
Recommended Use:
Cooperative Learning Activity
AL

Rail and Cyber Transportation
Strategy and Activity
Construction of railroads not only resulted in inexpensive and quick transport of goods, but also of people. Ask students how the ability to travel hundreds of miles a day may have affected European society. You should point out how today's e-mail affects society in much the same way that railroads did. E-mail enhances our ability to learn more about and potentially adopt another culture's customs, foods, dress, and so on. Ask students if they "chat" with anyone from another culture. If so, what have they learned? What motivated them to contact this person? Who do they believe benefits the most from these exchanges?

Rail and Cyber Transportation
Compare and Contrast
Recommended Use:
Chapter Introduction
OL

The Industrial Revolution
Role-Play
Recommended Use: Reteaching
AL

The Industrial Revolution
Strategy and Activity

Discuss with students the textbook's description of life in urban England and, in particular, life for the industrial working class during the mid-1800s. Have students consider the various aspects of daily life, including food, shelter, and working conditions in textile mills and coal mines. Next, ask students to imagine they are peasant landholders of England. Their family has farmed the same land for generations. Due to economic changes in the countryside, the family has lost its land and must move to find employment in a textile mill or coal mine. Have students write letters to a friend explaining how their family now lives: their home, their food, and their jobs. Which family members work? What are their various tasks? In their letters, have students compare this new life to the life they knew in the English countryside.

Drawing Parallels
Learning from Visuals
Recommended Use:
Independent Practice
OL

Drawing Parallels
Strategy and Activity

Ask students to find a picture of a family of freedmen living in the United States after the Civil War. Assign them to write a paragraph that compares the living conditions of this family and their prospects for the future with those of the Russian peasants shown in the photograph in the chapter "Industrialization and Nationalism." Why would both families have had little reason to be optimistic about their futures?

Romanticism v. Realism
Compare and Contrast
Recommended Use: Enrichment
EL

Romanticism v. Realism
Strategy and Activity

During the reading and discussion of Section 4 in the chapter "Industrialization and Nationalism," have the students make a chart with "Romanticism" and "Realism" as headings for the columns. As they read and discuss this section, students should list examples of people, works of art, and characteristics of romantics or realists. Under the heading "Romanticism," lists may include such characteristics as emotional, warm, sentimental, exotic, focused on inner feelings, unique, passionate, and interest in the past. Characteristics associated with "Realism" might include scientific, rational, ordinary, precise, harsh, and straightforward. Ask students to share their lists, comparing and contrasting the qualities of each view. Then have the students do a self-evaluation to answer the questions: "Am I more a romanticist or a realist? Why? What effect does that have on how I interact with people?"

Learn More About
Recognizing Points of View

Review with your class the information on the Franco-Prussian War. When did it occur? According to the Germans, what were the causes of the war? What were the causes of the war from the French viewpoint? What were the results of the war? *(Consider emotional as well as material results.)*

Following this review, have students write two articles. In the first article, they are to imagine they are Prussian historians writing an account of the war from the German perspective. In the second article, they are to imagine they are French historians and must write the article from the French viewpoint. In a class discussion, consider the accuracy of each viewpoint. Which, if either, represents the actual events? Why? If each nation regards its viewpoint as true history and teaches it to the next generation, what may happen?

German Unification—An In-Depth Activity

Background

After the Frankfurt Assembly failed to achieve German unification in 1848 and 1849, Germans looked to Prussia for leadership in the cause of German unification. In the course of the nineteenth century, Prussia had become a strong and prosperous state. Its government was authoritarian. The Prussian king had firm control over both the government and the army. Prussia was also known for its militarism, or reliance on military strength. In the 1860s, King William I tried to enlarge the Prussian army. When the Prussian legislature refused to levy new taxes for the proposed military changes, William I appointed a new prime minister, Count Otto von Bismarck. Bismarck has often been seen as the foremost nineteenth-century practitioner of *realpolitik*, the "politics of reality," or politics based on practical matters rather than on theory or ethics. Bismarck openly voiced his strong dislike of anyone who opposed him. After his appointment, he ignored the legislative opposition to the military reforms. He proceeded to collect taxes and strengthen the army. He followed an active foreign policy that soon led to the Franco-Prussian War. Eventually, the Prussian monarchy and the Prussian army created German unity, and the new German state became the strongest power on the European continent.

Strategy

Ask students to turn to page 869 in Glencoe Literature's *The Reader's Choice: World Literature* to read "The Lorelei" by Heinrich Heine, translated by Aaron Kramer. Explain to students that Heine came from a Jewish family in Düsseldorf and began his literary career while studying law at German universities. He left Germany for a time and joined French literary circles, but he is best known for his lyrical poems that brought a new tone of irony and skepticism to German literature. The Rhine River runs through Germany, and the Lorelei is a rock on the bank of this river. The rock produces an echo and grew to be associated with a legend about a beautiful woman who could lure sailors to their deaths with her beautiful singing:

> More lovely than a vision, A girl sits high up there;
> Her golden jewelry glistens,
> She combs her golden hair.
> With a comb of gold she combs it,
> And sings an evensong;
> The wonderful melody reaches
> A boat, as it sails along.
> The boatman hears, with an anguish
> More wild than was ever known;
> He's blind to the rocks around him;
> His eyes are for her alone.

"The Lorelei" gained great popularity in Germany, so much so that after anti-Semitic Nazis banned Heine's work because he was Jewish, this poem remained in schoolbooks with "anonymous" as its title.

Activities

Ask students the following questions, and then have them complete the activity that follows.

1. What is ironic about this poem? *(Things are not as they appear. The beautiful, golden woman tempts men and is pleased when they are destroyed.)*

2. "Gold" describes the jewelry, comb, and hair of the woman. How is this symbolic of her relationship to the boatmen? *(Because gold is all that touches this woman and is a commodity that is out of the reach of most common men, it is unrealistic for the boatmen to think they could actually touch her.)*

German Unification
Interdisciplinary Connection:
Language Arts
Skill: Analyze Literature
Recommended Use:
Team-Teaching Strategy
AL

3. **Writing Prompt** Ask students to use "The Lorelei" as the basis for a short story. Explain that the story should incorporate the setting, character, and conflict of the poem with additional details to create short prose writing. Students may wish to alter the tone of the poem in their stories by adding humor, surprise, gore, or tragedy. Allow students to share their writing aloud.

MASS SOCIETY AND DEMOCRACY

Key Terms and Reinforcement

Strategy and Activity

Compile a list of key terms for this chapter. Include words such as:

bourgeoisie   feminism
proletariat   literacy
dictatorship   psychoanalysis
revisionists   modernism

Ask students to complete a word web. Demonstrate for students the structure of a word web that includes the following components:

- word history
- related words
- synonyms
- antonyms
- part of speech
- dictionary definition
- original sentence using the word
- how the word relates to the chapter

As students encounter the word in the text, they should add to their word webs the sentence from the text that uses the word. Supply college-level dictionaries, thesauri, and word-origin dictionaries. Provide a model of the word web, using an overhead projector.

Learning About Economics

Strategy and Activity

Help students understand that growth in overall production does not necessarily mean all or most people have better lives. In 2005 the U.S. national income was $10,903.9 billion. Ask students to explain why this does not mean that each American household received a proportionate share ($96,370) of this money. Discuss with students the difference between "production" and "distribution" of wealth.

Social Commentary in Literature

Strategy and Activity

Have students read selections from Elizabeth Poole Sanford's *Woman in Her Social and Domestic Character* and Henrik Ibsen's *A Doll's House*. Have students compare the two attitudes toward women that are represented in the selections. Which viewpoint had the support of most men in the nineteenth century? Which one had the support of most women in the nineteenth century? How would a feminist from the early twentieth century react to the two selections? What biases and motivations are reflected in each work? Is either a completely accurate picture of the life of women in the nineteenth century? Complete the discussion by asking the class to review the descriptions in their textbooks of life for working-class women. To what extent would students be able to relate to either picture of a woman's life? How much sympathy would a poor working woman feel for Ibsen's Nora? How socially active could these women have been in the nineteenth century?

Internet Learning
Inventors

Have students visit the following URL, which contains an extensive list of inventors with a short history of their inventions. Edison, Bell, Marconi, and the Wright brothers are included. www. invent.org/hall_of_fame/1_0_0_hall_of_fame.asp

Pablo Picasso
*Point of View
Recommended Use:
Class Discussion
OL*

Pablo Picasso
Strategy and Activity

Show examples of Pablo Picasso's most famous paintings and ask students to discuss characteristics of his works. Many people appreciate Picasso's art and find it to be full of meaning. Many others find some of his paintings either too abstract or too confusing to understand. What explanations can students suggest for these differing points of view? Picasso entered Spain's School of Fine Arts at age 11. His early works were very realistic. His first large oil painting, which was displayed when Picasso was only 14 years old, was *First Communion,* an almost photographic and vibrant work. Try to obtain a copy of it to show your students. At the age of 17, Picasso decided to create the type of art for which he became famous. Ask students to consider this statement made by Picasso when he was 54 years old as an explanation for his cubist art: "A picture is not thought out and settled beforehand. While it is being done, it changes as one's thoughts change. And when it is finished, it goes on changing according to the state of mind of whomever is looking at it."

Learn More About
Kaiser William II

When 29-year-old William II ascended the imperial throne of Germany, a power struggle quickly developed with Prince Otto von Bismarck, national hero and unifier of Germany. Kaiser William wanted to rescind an order requiring Bismarck's permission before ministers conferred with the Kaiser. Rather than discussing this issue with the Kaiser, Bismarck changed the topic to the Kaiser's proposed visit with the Russian czar. Bismarck produced reports but refused to let the Kaiser read them. William grabbed one and found in it insulting comments about himself. Shortly afterwards, he asked Bismarck to resign. Bismarck later described William as "the man who will certainly ruin Germany."

Social Structure of the European Mass Society— An In-Depth Activity

Social Structure of the European
Mass Society
Interdisciplinary Connection:
Language Arts
Skill: Analyze Literature
Recommended Use:
Team-Teaching Strategy
AL

Background

By the end of the nineteenth century, the new European industrial world had led to the emergence of a mass society with more and more people living in cities. At the top of European society stood a wealthy elite. This group made up only 5 percent of the population but controlled from 30 to 40 percent of the wealth. Landed aristocrats, industrialists, bankers, and merchants made up this new elite. The middle classes consisted of a variety of groups. The upper middle class formed part of the new elite. The next layer consisted of doctors, lawyers, members of the civil service, business managers, engineers, architects, accountants, and chemists. Next came small shopkeepers, traders, and prosperous farmers. The final layer consisted of white-collar workers. Below the middles classes on the social scale were the working classes, which made up almost 80 percent of the European population. These classes included landholding peasants, farm laborers, and sharecroppers. Most people, including the working classes, enjoyed improved standards of living after 1870, when reforms created better living conditions in cities.

Strategy

Ask students to turn to page 951 in Glencoe Literature's *The Reader's Choice: World Literature* to read "The Bet" by Anton Chekhov, translated by Constance Garnett. Explain that Chekhov grew up in southern Russia and abhorred pretentiousness. He presents works that realistically examine the human relationships among the social classes and often creates portraits of a threatened upper class plagued by apathy. "The Bet" opens with a group of men debating the merits of both capital punishment and life imprisonment. When a 25-year-old lawyer is asked which punishment he considers to be the worst, he responds that "both are equally immoral, but if I had to choose between the death penalty and imprisonment for life, I would certainly choose the second. To live anyhow is better than not at all." This angers the banker, and he wages a bet the younger man cannot refuse, exclaiming, "It's not true! I'll bet you two millions you wouldn't stay in solitary confinement for five years." The younger man states that he will stay 15, the bet is agreed upon, and the young man is confined to a lodge in the banker's garden. The man spends his years reading, learning languages, playing music, and studying. As the end of the fifteenth year approaches, the banker is no longer extremely wealthy and is concerned about potential bankruptcy and disgrace. He determines that the imprisoned man must be killed before his release. He sneaks into the lodge where his prisoner is asleep and finds a note explaining that the prisoner has found wisdom in the books he read, and in turn he "despise[s] your books, I despise wisdom and the blessings of this world. It is all worthless, fleeting. . . . To prove . . . how I despise all that you live by . . . I shall go out from here five hours before the time fixed." The banker leaves without killing the lawyer, weeps, and feels great contempt for himself. The lawyer escapes what he hates—wealth—but also escapes death. In turn, the banker escapes poverty and disgrace. The reader is left to discover for himself the answer to the question that is the impetus for the story.

Activities

Ask students the following questions, and then have them complete the activity that follows.

1. How is the banker's life different at the end of the story? *(He is no longer wealthy, but he is basically the same pretentious character he was in the beginning of the story.)*

2. How is the lawyer different at the end of the story? *(His imprisonment changes him and alters who he is and how he thinks. He no longer believes that any kind of life is better than being dead.)*

3. **Writing Prompt** Ask students to write an opinion essay concerning the death penalty versus life imprisonment. Encourage students to research the modern and historic arguments concerning which provides the greater punishment, to develop and present an argument, and to use logical reasoning to support their opinion.

CHAPTER 21

THE HEIGHT OF IMPERIALISM

Key Terms and Reinforcement
Strategy and Activity

Compile a list of key terms for this chapter. Include words such as:

imperialism	sepoys
protectorate	viceroy
annexed	creoles
indigenous	

Ask students to complete a word web. Demonstrate for students the structure of a word web that includes the following components:

- word history
- related words
- synonyms
- antonyms
- part of speech
- dictionary definition
- original sentence using the word
- how the word relates to the chapter

As students encounter the word in the text, they should add to their word webs the sentence from the text that uses the word. Supply college-level dictionaries, thesauri, and word-origin dictionaries. Provide a model of the word web, using an overhead projector.

Key Terms and Reinforcement
Independent Practice Skill: Use Word Webs to Analyze Important Terms
Recommended Use: Reinforcement
OL

Colonial Legacy in Africa
Strategy and Activity

Organize the class into small groups, and assign each group to research a distinct area or country in Africa. Each group should research the dominant languages spoken today in its assigned region. How do areas where European languages are spoken correspond to the European conquest of Africa? Which countries show an overlap of African languages across their borders? What role did imperialism play in separating people of the same language into different countries? Where and why were different ethnic groups placed into the same country? Is there any relationship between arbitrary colonial divisions and war zones in modern Africa? When groups have finished their research, they should present the results (with illustrations and maps) to the entire class.

Colonial Legacy in Africa
Research and Create a Map
Recommended Use: Cooperative Learning
AL

Haiti
Strategy and Activity

You may wish to share some facts about modern-day Haiti with your students to reinforce their general geographic knowledge. Haiti is the world's first African-Caribbean republic in the Americas. It is also the poorest country in the Western Hemisphere. It was the second country in the Americas to achieve independence—thanks to the efforts of Toussaint L'Ouverture, who led the slave revolt against the French army there in 1801. (You will need to supply some background information about this event.) Unfortunately, the hopeful start promised by the 1801 constitution was never fulfilled, and the history of this country has been primarily one of repression and human-rights abuses. The literacy rate is only 53 percent, whereas unemployment figures are over 66 percent. About 80 percent of Haitians live in poverty. Artistically, Haiti is very advanced, and Haitian artists have developed a unique style employing vivid primary colors and strong emotional sentiments.

Haiti
Connecting Past and Present
Recommended Use: Enrichment
OL

Learn More About . . .
Lord Macauley

Although very influential in India, Lord Macauley is better known as a historian. His five-volume *History of England* was a very influential and much imitated work. The attitudes he displayed in India are also reflected in his histories—that English institutions were the best model for the colonies and that English standards of culture and society would be forever the norm for the world. Macauley stayed in India for only four years, but at an influential time when the British Crown was taking over government from the East India Company. He championed liberty of the press and equality before the law for Indians and Europeans. He also established the national education system based on Western principles to train an elite corps of Indians to serve the British Crown. Macauley, in his arrogance, could not foresee that the Indians would reject British rule in favor of nationalism.

What Makes an Enlightened Ruler?
Classroom Discussion
Recommended Use: Enrichment
EL

What Makes an Enlightened Ruler?
Strategy and Activity

Have students brainstorm characteristics that they believe would be associated with an "enlightened" ruler or ruling class. Students should draw on their knowledge of classical mythology, philosophical writings, their own personal value systems, and the characteristics they have learned about through their study of world history. After brainstorming, do a chip vote with the class, which is a method of winnowing down brainstorming options. Each student is allowed three votes—and the top six winners (depending upon the total number of options) are the consensus, or agreed upon, characteristics of an enlightened ruler.

Colonial Rule in Africa
Interdisciplinary Connection:
Language Arts
Skill: Analyze Literature
Recommended Use: Team-Teaching
Strategy
AL

Colonial Rule in Africa—An In-Depth Activity
Background

By 1914 Great Britain, France, Germany, Belgium, and Portugal had divided up Africa. Only Liberia, which had been created as a homeland for the formerly enslaved people of the United States, and Ethiopia remained free states. Native peoples who dared to resist were simply devastated by the Europeans' superior military force. Most European governments ruled their new territories in Africa with the least effort and expense possible. Indirect rule meant relying on existing political elites and institutions. The British especially followed this approach. In some areas, the British simply asked a local ruler to accept British authority and to fly the British flag over official buildings. The concept of indirect rule was introduced in the Islamic state of Sokoto, in northern Nigeria, beginning in 1903. This system of indirect rule in Sokoto had one good feature: it did not disrupt local customs and institutions. However, it did have some unfortunate consequences. The system was basically a fraud because British administrators made all major decisions. The native authorities served chiefly to enforce those decisions. Another problem was that indirect rule kept the old African elite in power. Such a policy provided few opportunities for ambitious and talented young Africans from outside the old elite. In this way, British indirect rule sowed the seeds for class and tribal tensions, which erupted after independence came in the twentieth century.

Strategy

Ask students to turn to page 129 in Glencoe Literature's *The Reader's Choice: World Literature* to read "The Voter" by Chinua Achebe. Achebe grew up in Ibo, a village in eastern Nigeria, and was the son of Christian missionary teachers. He became fascinated with his own people's customs and beliefs. Explain to students that Nigeria became an independent nation in 1960, and the efforts of the country to establish a democratic government were hampered by corrupt politicians and traditional hostilities stemming from imperial rule. Achebe's story is set in Ibo shortly after independence and focuses on the central character of Roof, who has been employed by Honorable Marcus Ibe. Marcus Ibe began his political career as a mission teacher of questionable character. He was elected to office and now "he had two long cars and had just built himself the biggest house anyone had seen in these parts." Furthermore, although the village did not have running water or electricity, "he had lately installed a private plant to supply electricity to his new house."

The villagers praise Ibe, but they also recognize that "they had underrated the power of the ballot paper and should not do so again." As Ibe's employee, Roof finds that the ballots he purchased from villagers during the reelection cost Ibe much more than during the first election. Then the leader of the opposing party visits Roof and bribes him to cast his vote for Maduka, Ibe's challenger. When faced with actually casting his vote, Roof falters, then tears his paper in half and places one half in each box, being careful to take "precaution of putting the first half into Maduka's box and confirming the action verbally." The story concludes with Roof exiting the voting "booth as jauntily as he had gone in."

Activities

Ask students the following questions, and then have them complete the activity that follows.

1. How does public office change Ibe's life? *(His salary changes his lifestyle. It permits him to have great luxuries.)*

2. Why does the author have Roof accept a bribe? *(to emphasize the extent of the political corruption and financial deprivation in Africa following independence)*

3. **Writing Prompt** Ask students to consider the political problems magnified by "The Voter." Ask them to assume that they are consultants hired to analyze the corrupt politics in the village and then to write a plan the villagers can follow to clean up their political campaigns.

EAST ASIA UNDER CHALLENGE

Key Terms and Reinforcement

Strategy and Activity

Compile a list of key terms for this chapter. Include words such as:

extraterritoriality	commodities
spheres of influence	concessions
indemnity	prefectures
provincial	

Ask students to complete a word web. Demonstrate for students the structure of a word web that includes the following components:

- word history
- related words
- synonyms
- antonyms
- part of speech
- dictionary definition
- original sentence using the word
- how the word relates to the chapter

As students encounter the word in the text, they should add to their word webs the sentence from the text that uses the word. Supply college-level dictionaries, thesauri, and word-origin dictionaries. Provide a model of the word web, using an overhead projector.

"Western" Influences in Japan

Strategy and Activity

Direct students to Section 3 of the chapter "East Asia Under Challenge." During the time of the Meiji Restoration, a conscious effort was made to imitate Western culture. The Japanese government called this process "civilization and enlightenment." Western culture, from intellectual trends to clothing and architecture, were widely promoted. Ask students to discuss how the images in this section reflect Western culture. (*Answers could include Western dress, hairstyles, sports, dance, and eating habits.*)

Prejudice and Racism

Strategy and Activity

To illustrate that prejudice and racism affect the climate of world affairs, remind students that the Japanese in America suffered discrimination before World War I. Reacting to Japanese immigration in the late 1890s and early 1900s, Californians in 1905 organized a Japanese and Korean Exclusion League to combat the "Japanese menace." In 1906 a San Francisco school board assigned all Asian students to one segregated school. The Japanese government protested this slur to the government. Have students research and write an essay on how Theodore Roosevelt negotiated with the Japanese to resolve the problem.

Key Terms and Reinforcement
Independent Practice Skill: Use Word Webs to Analyze Important Terms
Recommended Use: Reinforcement
OL

"Western" Influences in Japan
Compare and Contrast
Recommended Use: Introducing Concepts
BL

Prejudice and Racism
Identifying Central Issues
Recommended Use: Enrichment
BL

Learn More About . . .
The Boxer Rebellion

The multinational force that put down the Boxer Rebellion included soldiers from Japan, France, Germany, Great Britain, and the United States. The indemnity that the Chinese government had to pay to these Western nations was $333 million. Of that sum, $24.5 million was to go to the United States. When the United States government realized that this was far more than the expense for its troops and the damages caused from the fighting, it reimbursed the Chinese government $18 million. This money was then set aside by the Chinese to send students to study in America. These students would eventually help to bring American ideas to China.

Balance of Trade
Introducing Concepts
Recommended Use: Enrichment
OL

Balance of Trade
Strategy and Activity

Explain what a trade imbalance is. Tell students that trade imbalance is still an important issue in international trade and international relations. Ask students why a trade imbalance is regarded as harmful to a nation's economy. *(A country pays out more money for imports than it receives from its exports.)* To reinforce the idea of imbalance, ask students to list the products they own that were made in China. Then remind students that the Chinese purchase few American products. Ask: How is this similar to the British response to China? *(Both tried to balance trade by increasing exports.)*

The Meiji Restoration
Interdisciplinary Connection:
Language Arts
Skill: Analyze Literature
Recommended Use: Team-Teaching
Strategy
AL

The Meiji Restoration—An In-Depth Activity
Background

The Sat-Cho leaders had genuinely mistrusted the West, but they soon realized that Japan must change to survive. The new leaders embarked on a policy of reform, transforming Japan into a modern industrial nation. The symbol of the new era was the young emperor Mutsuhito. The period of his reign became known as the Meiji Restoration. Japanese society before the Meiji reforms could be described by two words: *community* and *hierarchy*. The lives of all Japanese people were determined by their membership in a family, village, and social class. Women were especially limited by the "three obediences": child to father, wife to husband, and widow to son. Husbands could easily obtain a divorce; wives could not. Marriages were arranged, and the average marital age of females was 16 years. The Meiji Restoration had a marked effect on the traditional social system in Japan. Western fashions and culture became the rage. The ministers of the first Meiji government were known as the "dancing cabinet" because they loved Western-style ballroom dancing. A new generation of modern boys and girls began to imitate the clothing styles, eating habits, hairstyles, and social practices of European and American young people.

Strategy

Ask students to turn to page 652 in Glencoe Literature's *The Reader's Choice: World Literature* to read "The Jay" by Yasunari Kawabata. Explain to the students that this story is set in Japan in 1940. Yoshiko is the central character who lives with her brother and aging grandmother. Her father and stepmother moved from the house after Yoshiko's brother discovered and wanted to meet their birth mother, whom their father had divorced because she "went around dressed in flashy clothes and spent money wildly." Although the stepmother said, "It's a good thing, a good thing. It's not bad to meet your own mother. It's only natural," Yoshiko noticed that during the conversation the "strength seemed to have gone out of her stepmother's body." Thus, the father and stepmother left the home, and "when her father, who had moved away from her, came back bringing a marriage proposal, Yoshiko had been surprised." Concerned that there would be no one to care for her brother and blind grandmother if she left, Yoshiko made up her mind to accept the proposal when "it had been decided that the two households would become one." A subplot is woven into this story involving a mother jaybird calling constantly for her chick that had fallen from the nest. Yoshiko is impressed by her blind grandmother who interprets what is going on with the birds in spite of her inability to view the scene. When Yoshiko finds the baby bird, she follows her grandmother's calm advice to give it water and then return it to its mother. Yoshiko wishes that her father and stepmother were there to see the joyous reunion of the jays.

Activities

Ask students the following questions, and then have them complete the activity that follows.

1. Why does Yoshiko wish her father and stepmother were there to see the reunion of the birds? *(Yoshiko sees the reunion between the birds and wishes such a reunion were possible for her brother, mother, and herself.)*

2. Given the problems faced by her father in his first marriage, do you think Yoshiko is anxious to marry? *(Yoshiko's father allowed her to choose to accept or decline the proposal. She understands her traditional role and is relieved her grandmother and brother will continue to live with her.)*

3. **Writing Prompt** Ask students to write an essay identifying and explaining the benefits and risks of an arranged marriage. Ask them to conclude the essay by describing the requirements they would include in a marriage contract if their parents were to arrange a marriage for them.

WAR AND REVOLUTION

Key Terms and Reinforcement

Strategy and Activity

Compile a list of key terms for this chapter. Include words such as:

conscription	soviets
mobilization	armistice
propaganda	reparations
total war	mandates

Ask students to complete a word web. Demonstrate for students the structure of a word web that includes the following components:

- word history
- related words
- synonyms
- antonyms
- part of speech
- dictionary definition
- original sentence using the word
- how the word relates to the chapter

As students encounter the word in the text, they should add to their word webs the sentence from the text that uses the word. Supply college-level dictionaries, thesauri, and word-origin dictionaries. Provide a model of the word web, using an overhead projector.

Patriot or Nationalist?

Strategy and Activity

Ask students to consider the differences between patriots and nationalists. On the board, write the heading "Attitude." Underneath, list topics such as: toward own country, toward other countries, toward own armies, toward own expansion, toward others' expansion, toward own leaders, toward other leaders. Beside the list, create a two-column chart of comparison, using the headings "Patriot" and "Nationalist." Have students brainstorm patriotic and nationalistic attitudes. Afterward, under the heading "Behavior," have students brainstorm possible patriotic and nationalistic behaviors stemming from the listed attitudes.

Technological Advances

Strategy and Activity

An unprecedented number of new machines and devices were first used on a large scale during World War I. These included submarines, airplanes, tanks, motor trucks, machine guns, rapid-fire artillery, barbed wire, and poison gas. Organize students into groups to complete a project (paper, visual display, oral report, and so on) that chronicles the development of a technological advance of World War I. Have students define the task thoroughly and assign roles and responsibilities. After the project is completed, the group should evaluate each member's contribution, highlighting aspects of the work that went well and suggesting ways the team might have functioned better.

Key Terms and Reinforcement
Independent Practice Skill: Use Word Webs to Analyze Important Terms
Recommended Use: Reinforcement
OL

Patriot or Nationalist?
Compare and Contrast
Recommended Use: Class Discussion
EL

Technological Advances
Understanding Cause and Effect
Recommended Use: Cooperative Learning Activity
BL

Understanding New Vocabulary
Expanding Vocabulary
Recommended Use: Enrichment
EL

Understanding New Vocabulary

Strategy and Activity

Many words we use today have their roots in World War I. Some examples include:

Ace: originally a pilot who shot down five enemy planes; later came to mean anyone who was exceptionally good at something

Chow: originally from the Chinese word *ch'ao* (to cook), soldiers used it to describe military food; soldiers themselves were called **chowhounds**

Civvies: originally a British soldier's term for nonmilitary (civilian) clothing

Doughboys: a term, the origin of which is unclear, referring to American soldiers

Dud: originally a bomb that did not go off; later a person who did not perform

Rookie: from the word *recruit,* it meant a new soldier; later used to describe anyone who was inexperienced

Ask students how many of these words they are familiar with and how they have used them. Do any of these words have other meanings in today's usage? (An *ace* is also an unreturned serve in most net sports, for example.) Are they surprised at the derivation of these common words?

Peace Treaties
Making Connections
Recommended Use: Enrichment
BL

Peace Treaties

Strategy and Activity

Explain to students that the mishandling of the peace settlements of World War I led directly to World War II. Have students list ways in which the Paris Peace Conference and the Versailles peace treaty were mishandled. Then discuss the relative importance and possible results of each item on the list.

European Powers at War
Interdisciplinary Connection:
Language Arts
Skill: Analyze Literature
Recommended Use: Team-Teaching
Strategy
AL

European Powers at War—An In-Depth Activity

Background

Militarism, nationalism, and the desire to stifle internal dissent all played a role in the starting of World War I. However, the decisions made by European leaders in response to another crisis in the Balkans in the summer of 1914 led directly to the conflict. Serbia wanted a large, independent Slavic state in the Balkans, and Austria-Hungary was adamantly opposed to this. When Archduke Ferdinand was assassinated, Austria-Hungary saw an opportunity to forcefully render Serbia harmless. Fearful of the Russians, Austria-Hungary sought and received Germany's full support. Eventually, Austria-Hungary declared war on Serbia. Russia, which supported Serbia's causes, could not mobilize against Austria-Hungary only, so the czar ordered full mobilization, which Germany considered an act of war. Germany proposed an ultimatum demanding that Russia cease its mobilization efforts and declared war after Russia ignored the ultimatum. Following the Schleiffen Plan, Germany declared war on France. Great Britain, concerned with maintaining its own world power, responded by declaring war on Germany for violating Belgian neutrality. Soon, all the great powers of Europe were at war.

Strategy

Ask students to turn to page 971 in Glencoe Literature's *The Reader's Choice: World Literature* to read "The Panther" by Rainer Maria Rilke. Explain to students that Rilke was born in Prague, which was part of the Austrian Empire. He spoke and usually wrote in German. Although the poem is not necessarily political in nature, encourage students to consider how the caged panther in the poem represents the members of mass society who are "caged" when nations engage in war, whether in agreement or dissension with governmental decisions:

His vision, from the constant passing bars has grown so weary that it cannot hold anything else. It seems to him there are a thousand bars; and behind the bars, no world.

Ask students to consider how the panther's intensely fleeting interest in the world beyond his cage often mirrors the collective interest of a warring society in the world beyond its turmoil:

Only at times, the curtain of the pupils lifts, quietly—. An image enters in, rushes down through the tensed, arrested muscles, plunges into the heart and is gone.

Activities

Ask students the following questions, and then have them complete the activity below.

1. How is the caged panther's world similar to that of the mass society of a warring nation? *(The panther is caught; there is no escape. People involved in war often feel the same.)*

2. How is the caged panther's perspective similar to the perspective of the people of warring nations? *(His cage limits the panther's perspective, so much so that he begins to believe that nothing more than his reality exists. Such is often the case among the people of warring countries).*

3. **Writing Prompt** Ask students to identify controversial decisions recently enacted by the local, state, or federal government. After discussion and research of a specific action, ask students to analyze the potential positive and negative effects the decision will have on society on both a limited and expansive scale.

THE WEST BETWEEN THE WARS

Key Terms and Reinforcement

Strategy and Activity

Compile a list of key terms for this chapter. Include words such as:

Depression
collective bargaining
totalitarian state
fascism

collectivization
concentration camp
surrealism

Ask students to complete a word web. Demonstrate for students the structure of a word web that includes the following components:

- word history
- related words
- synonyms
- antonyms
- part of speech
- dictionary definition
- original sentence using the word
- how the word relates to the chapter

As students encounter the word in the text, they should add to their word webs the sentence from the text that uses the word. Supply college-level dictionaries, thesauri, and word-origin dictionaries. Provide a model of the word web, using an overhead projector.

Key Terms and Reinforcement
Independent Practice Skill: Use Word Webs to Analyze Important Terms
Recommended Use: Reinforcement
OL

The Depression Era

Strategy and Activity

Ask interested students to bring in recordings (if possible) or words of Depression-era songs. A good example is Woody Guthrie's "Brother, Can You Spare a Dime?" but there are many others available as well. What effect do students think these songs had on people struggling to survive? Would these songs be called "protest songs"? Why does music often reflect the social climate in which it is written?

The Depression Era
Compare and Contrast
Recommended Use: Cross Curriculum—Music
OL

Emergence of Extremism

Strategy and Activity

Discuss with students the relationship between the Great Depression and the rise of extremist groups throughout the world. Have students list the factors that made people favor extremist political parties in a time of economic disaster. (Answers might include but will not be limited to unemployment, social discontent, fear of the future, fear of the unemployed masses, fear of communism, desire for a strong government to solve the economic problems or to protect property holders.) Which social groups would have been swayed by which factors? How did the various governments discussed in Chapter 24 meet these factors? Ask students to research and write an essay in which they discuss how the Great Depression opened the door to extremist political parties in Italy, Germany, Spain, and Japan. What specific factors were involved, and what economic group provided the greatest support for the extremist government?.

Emergence of Extremism
Classroom Discussion
Recommended Use: Enrichment
BL

Copyright © Glencoe/McGraw-Hill, a division of The McGraw-Hill Companies, Inc.

More About Mass Reactions
Research
Recommended Use: Independent Reading
AL

More About Mass Reactions
Strategy and Activity

The use of cinema for propaganda purposes is thoroughly examined in D. Welch's *Propaganda and the German Cinema* (New York, 1985). The organization of leisure time in Fascist Italy is thoughtfully discussed in V. De Grazia's *The Culture of Consent: Mass Organization of Leisure in Fascist Italy* (New York, 1981). For the cultural and intellectual environment of Weimar Germany, see W. Laqueur's *Weimar: A Cultural History* (New York, 1974); and P. Gray's *Weimar Culture: The Outsider as Insider* (New York, 1968). For a study of Carl Jung, see G. Wehr's *Jung: A Biography* (New York, 1987).

People & Places
Joseph Stalin

Joseph Stalin was born Iosif Vissarionovich Dzhugashvili in 1879, but adopted the pseudonym Stalin in about 1910. Stalin means "a man of steel." As a schoolboy in Gori, which is in the Republic of Georgia, Stalin was forced to learn Russian even though neither of his parents spoke it. Stalin was the best student in the church school he attended and, as such, earned a full scholarship to a theological seminary.

While in the seminary, Stalin read forbidden literature, especially the works of Karl Marx. Before long, Stalin converted to Russian Marxism. He eventually quit the seminary to become a full-time revolutionary.

Stalin joined the Social-Democratic Party, which was a Marxist revolutionary group. While part of this group, he spread propaganda among railroad workers. He was arrested, spent a year in prison, and then was exiled to Siberia. He eventually escaped from Siberia. However, the pattern of arrest, imprisonment, and exile became common to Stalin. Over the next several years, he was arrested eight times, exiled seven times, and escaped six times. His last arrest was for helping to organize a bank robbery. This time the government was able to contain him in exile for four years.

Stalin became an important figure in the Social-Democratic Party and began writing as editor of the party newspaper, *Pravda*. His first important published work was *Marxism and the Nationality Question*. His organizational skills strengthened his position in the party and, on Lenin's death, Stalin was able to join with Kamenev and Zinovyev to lead the country.

Literature Between the Wars
Sharing Literature
Recommended Use: Classroom Discussion
BL

Literature Between the Wars
Strategy and Activity

T. S. Eliot, an Anglo-American poet, spoke for many of his generation about the decay of Western culture in his poem "The Waste Land." In another poem, "The Hollow Men," he writes of the despair many felt with the lack of purpose of the "lost generation."

> We are the hollow men
> We are the stuffed men
> Learning together
> Headpiece filled with straw. Alas!
> Our dried voices, when
> We whisper together
> Are quiet and meaningless . . .

An Irish poet, W. B. Yeats was prophetic in his poem "The Second Coming." In retrospect, his images almost provide a warning of the rise of Hitler, as well as the failure of the appeasement of the West to stop fascism.

> Things fall apart; the centre cannot hold
> Mere anarchy is loosed upon the world.
> The blood-dimmed tide is loosed, and everywhere
> The ceremony of innocence is drowned;
> The best lack all conviction, while the worst
>
> Are full of passionate intensity.

Ask for volunteers to read these selections aloud. Then direct the discussion toward recognizing literature as a reflection of the society in which the authors lived.

The Spanish Civil War—An In-Depth Activity

Background

It seemed that political democracy would become well established in eastern Europe after World War I. Many European states adopted parliamentary systems. However, authoritarian regimes soon replaced most of these systems. Parliamentary systems failed in most eastern European states for several reasons. These states had little tradition of political democracy. In addition, they were mostly rural and agrarian. Many of the peasants were illiterate, and much of the land was still dominated by large landowners who feared the peasants. Ethnic conflicts also plagued these countries. In Spain, too, political democracy failed to survive. Spanish military forces, led by General Francisco Franco, revolted against the democratic government in 1936. A brutal and bloody civil war began, complicated by foreign intervention. The fascist regimes of Italy and Germany aided Franco's forces. Hitler used the Spanish Civil War as an opportunity to test the new weapons of his revived air force. The Spanish Civil War came to an end when Franco's forces captured Madrid in 1939. Franco established a dictatorship that favored large landowners, business people, and the Catholic clergy. Because it favored traditional groups and did not try to control every aspect of people's lives, Franco's dictatorship was authoritarian rather than totalitarian.

Strategy

Ask students to turn to page 991 in Glencoe Literature's *The Reader's Choice: World Literature* to read "The Guitar" by Federico García Lorca. Explain to students that Lorca was one of Spain's greatest modern writers. He was raised in the countryside of Andalusia in southern Spain and reached the height of his career in the 1930s. Although he was not a political writer, his writings offended conservative Spaniards. When social tensions erupted into civil war in 1936, Lorca was arrested and shot by the right-wing Nationalists. Music was an important part of Lorca's life, and his style in this poem involves the use of figurative language to stir in the reader the moods evoked by a guitar:

> The crying of the guitar starts . . . It is crying for things far off. The warm sand of the South that asks for white camellias. For the arrow with nothing to hit, the evening with no dawn coming, and the first bird of all dead on the branch.

The author states that the music of the guitar "cries" "as the water cries, as the wind cries over the snow."

The Spanish Civil War
Interdisciplinary Connection:
Language Arts
Skill: Analyze Literature
Recommended Use: Team-Teaching
Strategy
AL

Activities

Ask students the following questions, and then have them complete the activity below.

1. What mood is evoked in the reader when the writer personifies the guitar by saying it cries? *(The mood is mournful, sorrowful, or wishful.)*

2. Why does the guitar cry? *(The guitar cries for what it cannot have.)*

3. **Writing Prompt** Ask students to bring their favorite instrumental recordings to class, or invite the musicians in the class to play their favorite instrumental piece. Ask students to use similes and metaphors to describe the music to someone who has never heard the piece.

CHAPTER 25

NATIONALISM AROUND THE WORLD

Key Terms and Reinforcement

Strategy and Activity

Compile a list of key terms for this chapter. Include words such as:

genocide   *zaibatsu*
ethnic cleansing   redistribution of wealth
Pan-Africanism   oligarchy
civil disobedience

Ask students to complete a word web. Demonstrate for students the structure of a word web that includes the following components:

- word history
- related words
- synonyms
- antonyms
- part of speech
- dictionary definition
- original sentence using the word
- how the word relates to the chapter

As students encounter the word in the text, they should add to their word webs the sentence from the text that uses the word. Supply college-level dictionaries, thesauri, and word-origin dictionaries. Provide a model of the word web, using an overhead projector.

American Intervention in Latin America

Strategy and Activity

American interventionism in Latin America has had mixed results. Often American actions have been rewarded with the "right" general in power, or the "right" political posture (that is, pro-United States). In the long term, however, most experts agree that American intervention—whether overtly militaristic or covertly through the CIA—has cost the country more than it has gained. Instead of becoming the leader of the Americas by example, American intervention has created resentment and suspicion. As a result, the United States today has more diplomatic clout in Europe than it has in its own backyard. Ask students if they think today's diplomacy is doing anything to make our Latin American neighbors perceive the United States as a "cooperative neighbor" instead of as a "big brother." Could new treaties such as NAFTA and cooperative efforts to stop drug traffic be changing perceptions to the better? Why or why not?

Learn More About . . .
Mohandas Gandhi

Mohandas Gandhi led India to independence and showed the world the effectiveness of passive civil disobedience. The disciples of Gandhi forswore aggression, even in self-defense. The outcome was that the aggressors could no longer bear the weight of inflicting pain on peaceful, passive energy. Gandhi's example was followed by Martin Luther King Jr. in the 1960s in the United States. The moral force of passive civil disobedience proved itself—as in Gandhi's India—powerful enough to dismantle institutional discrimination and bring civil rights to millions of Americans. Gandhi and his nation achieved what traditional force might not have achieved. Encourage students to talk about passive resistance they may have seen during their lifetimes. Ask if any of them have participated in a peaceful demonstration or would do so for a cause in which they believe.

Key Terms and Reinforcement
*Independent Practice Skill: Use Word Webs to Analyze Important Terms
Recommended Use: Reinforcement
OL*

American Intervention in Latin America
*Identifying Central Issues
Recommended Use: Enrichment
BL*

National Heroes
Point of View
Recommended Use: Cooperative
Learning Activity
EL

National Heroes
Strategy and Activity

Ask students to brainstorm words they think of when they hear the word *hero*. Then organize the class into small groups. Give them 10 minutes to discuss why nationalist feelings (such as strong allegiance to one's own country, or dislike of foreign presence) tend to inspire heroic leaders. Have each group select a member to list its words on the board. After each group has written its list, circle the common words that might indicate a consensus on what constitutes a hero.

The Long March
Interdisciplinary Connection:
Language Arts
Skill: Analyze Literature
Recommended Use: Team-Teaching
Strategy
AL

The Long March—An In-Depth Activity
Background

Revolutionary Marxism had its greatest impact on China. By 1920 central authority had almost ceased to exist in China. Two political forces began to emerge as competitors for the right to rule China: Sun Yat-sen's Nationalist Party, which had been driven from the political arena several years earlier, and the Chinese Communist Party. For more than three years, the two parties overlooked their mutual suspicions and worked together, but eventually tensions between the parties rose to the surface. Chiang Kai-shek succeeded Sun Yat-sen as the head of the Nationalist Party and pretended to support the alliance with the Communists. In April 1927, however, he struck against the Communists and their supporters in Shanghai, killing thousands in what is called the Shanghai Massacre. After the massacre, most of the Communist leaders went into hiding in Shanghai and recruited Communists among the working class. Chiang began to root Communist leaders from their strongholds in Shanghai and Jiangxi Province, and surrounded the base in Jiangxi in 1934. Mao Zedong, the new young Communist leader, and his army, the People's Liberation Army (PLA), broke through the Nationalist lines and began its famous Long March. Mao's army marched almost 6,000 miles to reach the last surviving Communist base in northwest China. Of the 90,000 troops who had embarked on the journey, only 9,000 remained. In the course of the Long March, Mao Zedong had become the sole leader of the Chinese Communist Party. To the people who lived at the time, it must have seemed that the Communist threat was over. To the Communists, however, hope remained for the future.

Strategy

Ask students to turn to page 645 in Glencoe Literature's *The Reader's Choice: World Literature* to read "The Long March" by Mao Tse-tung (also spelled Zedong). Explain to students that Mao took command of the Long March. Despite the great loss of life suffered by the PLA (also known as the Red Army), the Long March was a great victory for the Communists and for Mao. Many young Chinese were inspired to join the Communist Party, and Mao emerged as the undisputed party leader, perhaps in part due to his optimism. Ask students to consider these lines from Mao's poem:

> None in the Red Army feared the distresses of the Long March.
> We looked lightly on the ten thousand peaks and ten thousand rivers. . . .
>
> Delighting in the thousand snowy folds of the Ming Mountains,
> The last pass vanquished, the Three Armies smiled.

Activities

Ask students the following questions, and then have them complete the activity below.

1. What words and phrases speak to the positive attitude of the Red Army concerning the Long March? *(none feared, looked lightly on ten thousand peaks, delighting in the thousand snowy folds, Three Armies smiled)*

2. Why is the reaction of the Three Armies ironic? *(They lost hundreds of thousands of comrades. One would expect the army to be depressed and remorseful.)*

3. **Writing Prompt** The Red Army faced and overcame an incredibly difficult obstacle. Ask students to write a personal narrative about an obstacle they faced and overcame, either as an individual or as a part of a group. Allow students to share their writing aloud.

Key Terms and Reinforcement

Strategy and Activity

Compile a list of key terms for this chapter. Include words such as:

appeasement	genocide
demilitarized	collaborators
sanctions	mobilization
blitzkrieg	kamikaze
partisans	

Ask students to complete a word web. Demonstrate for students the structure of a word web that includes the following components:

- word history
- related words
- synonyms
- antonyms
- part of speech
- dictionary definition
- original sentence using the word
- how the word relates to the chapter

As students encounter the word in the text, they should add to their word webs the sentence from the text that uses the word. Supply college-level dictionaries, thesauri, and word-origin dictionaries. Provide a model of the word web, using an overhead projector.

Location, Location, Location

Strategy and Activity

Ask students to consider Japan and its foreign policy of expansion in the 1930s and 1940s. The economic geography of Japan—the economic resources contained within its borders—was a serious limitation of the Japanese aim to become a great power. Japan felt that it had to gain access to the resources for a modern industrial economy. This meant expansion toward Korea, China, the Soviet Union, and the adjoining Pacific areas. A weakness in economic geography directly led to aggression and imperialism. Today Japan has found a peaceful way to meet the demands created by a lack of natural resources: import and export. Through exports, Japan can afford to buy natural resources in the world market.

People & Places
Leaders at Yalta

Have students evaluate the effectiveness of each of the three leaders at Yalta: Franklin Delano Roosevelt, United States; Winston Churchill, Great Britain; and Joseph Stalin, Soviet Union. How much difference do students believe these men made in the course of World War II as individuals? How responsible was each for the course of the war and the postwar changes that occurred in the late 1940s? Students should use their textbooks for basic information concerning these men and their roles at Yalta and then examine other sources such as encyclopedias, biographies, and the Internet to formulate their opinions.

Key Terms and Reinforcement
Independent Practice Skill: Use Word Webs to Analyze Important Terms
Recommended Use: Reinforcement
OL

Location, Location, Location
Understanding Cause and Effect
Recommended Use: Classroom Discussion
BL

Women at War
Strategy and Activity

Although women did not serve as soldiers during World War II, they did serve in the military. In the United States, the Women's Army Corps (WAC) was established in 1942 as the Women's Auxiliary Army Corps, and more than 99,000 women served in this unit alone. American women also served in a unit of the U.S. Navy, the Women Accepted for Volunteer Emergency Service (WAVES). In 1948 both the WAC and WAVES became a regular part of the military. Have students research the roles of women in all of the warring countries. How did their roles differ from men, and how did their roles differ from country to country? You may wish to ask students to address the opportunities that World War II created for women on the home front as well as in the military.

Learn More About . . .
Hitler the General

Part of the mythological picture of Adolf Hitler is that he was considered a great military strategist. The following examples partially show the folly of such thoughts. Without subduing Britain, Hitler initiated an attack against the Soviet Union, creating a two-front war. He seriously underestimated Soviet capability. Prior to D-Day, the Allies led Hitler into believing that the invasion of Europe would take place at Calais. When the attack came on Normandy, he delayed the redeployment of his forces. By the time his troops became active, it was too late.

Learn More About . . .
Elie Wiesel, Auschwitz Survivor

Students might be interested in the background and writings of Elie Wiesel, one of the few to survive the Auschwitz concentration camp. Wiesel's parents were both killed in concentration camps. He moved to Paris after the war, where he studied at the University of Paris and worked as a newspaper correspondent. In 1963 Wiesel became a citizen of the United States, and from 1980 to 1986, Wiesel was chairman of the President's Commission on the Holocaust. He received the Congressional Medal of Honor in 1985 and the Nobel Peace Prize in 1986 for his work in promoting human rights. In his book *Night*, Wiesel describes his experiences at Auschwitz. Other writings include *Dawn*, *The Accident*, *The Town Beyond the Wall*, *A Beggar in Jerusalem*, *The Testament*, and *The Forgotten*.

Students might also be interested in visiting The Elie Wiesel Foundation for Humanity Web site, www.eliewieselfoundation.org, to learn more about Wiesel's continuing humanitarian activities.

Internet Learning
Nuremberg War Crime Trials

Direct students to the following URL, where they will find information and additional Web site resources to enhance their study of the Nuremberg War Crimes Trials. This site leads to a complete accounting of the trials, how they were run, and who was tried. www.yale.edu/lawweb/avalon/imt/imt.htm

The Holocaust—An In-Depth Activity

Background

Hitler's plans for an Aryan racial empire were so important to him that he and the Nazis began to put their racial program into effect soon after the Polish conquest. One million Poles were uprooted and moved to southern Poland, while hundreds of thousands of ethnic Germans were brought in to colonize the German provinces in Poland. Hitler's plans included removing Poles, Ukrainians, and Russians from their lands to become slave labor. German peasants would then settle on the abandoned lands and "Germanize" them. No aspect of the Nazi New Order was more terrifying than the deliberate attempt to exterminate the Jews. Racial struggle was a key element in Hitler's world of ideas. On one side were the Aryans, creators of human cultural development. On the other side were the Jews, who Hitler believed were trying to destroy the Aryans. Heinrich Himmler and the SS shared Hitler's racial ideas. The SS was given responsibility for what the Nazis called their Final Solution—genocide of the Jewish people.

Strategy

Ask students to turn to page 1001 in Glencoe Literature's *The Reader's Choice: World Literature* to read from *Night* by Elie Wiesel. Explain that Wiesel lived in Romania until 1944 when, at age 14, Weisel was one of the Jews rounded up by Nazi soldiers for extermination. The Weisel family was transported by train to Auschwitz, a German concentration camp where more than 800,000 Jews died, mostly in gas chambers designed for mass genocide. Wiesel's mother and sister died in this camp before Weisel and his father were transferred to Buchenwald, a camp within Germany that sent prisoners to work in nearby weapons plants. Although there were no gas chambers at Buchenwald, many prisoners died from disease, exhaustion, beatings, and executions, or a combination thereof.

> "Quiet, over there!" yelled the officer.
>
> "Eliezer," went on my father [who was feeble, exhausted, and suffering from dysentery], "some water. . . ."
>
> The officer came up to him and shouted at him to be quiet. . . . He went on calling me. The officer dealt him a violent blow on the head with his truncheon.
>
> When I got down after roll call, I could see his lips trembling as he murmured something. Bending over him, I stayed gazing at him for over an hour, engraving into myself the picture of his blood-stained face, his shattered skull.
>
> I awoke [the next morning] at dawn. In my father's place lay another invalid.

Wiesel's depiction of Jewish persecution is stark and riveting, as is his honesty about his father's death:

> I did not weep. . . . I had no more tears. . . . In the recesses of my weakened conscience . . . I might perhaps have found something like—free at last!

The Holocaust
Interdisciplinary Connection:
Language Arts
Skill: Analyze Literature
Recommended Use: Team-Teaching
Strategy
AL

Activities

Ask students the following questions, and then have them complete the activity below.

1. Describe how this excerpt makes you feel. *(Answers will vary.)*

2. State the possible double meanings of Wiesel's last words in the excerpt. *(Perhaps he was referring to his father who found freedom in death; perhaps he was referring to himself since protecting and caring for his suffering father would no longer encumber him.)*

3. **Writing Prompt** Ask students to collect biographical information about Jews who were either victims or survivors of the Nazis. Use the information to create a wall of remembrance and tribute.

Differentiated Instruction for the World History Classroom

CHAPTER 27

COLD WAR AND POSTWAR CHANGES

Key Terms and Reinforcement

Strategy and Activity

Compile a list of key terms for this chapter. Include words such as:

satellite states	de-Stalinization
arms race	welfare state
deterrence	bloc
domino theory	real wages

Ask students to complete a word web. Demonstrate for students the structure of a word web that includes the following components:

- word history
- related words
- synonyms
- antonyms
- part of speech
- dictionary definition
- original sentence using the word
- how it relates to the chapter

As students encounter the word in the text, they should add to their word webs the sentence from the text that uses the word. Supply college-level dictionaries, thesauri, and word-origin dictionaries. Provide a model of the word web, using an overhead projector.

Key Terms and Reinforcement
Independent Practice Skill: Use Word Webs to Analyze Important Terms
Recommended Use: Reinforcement
OL

Personal Freedoms

Strategy and Activity

After World War II, what differences developed between the personal freedoms enjoyed by most people in Western Europe and those given to people who lived in Eastern Europe? How did this affect relations between Eastern European nations of the Soviet bloc and the West? Help students understand that most people in Western Europe enjoyed personal freedoms and had a voice in their governments. In Eastern Europe, however, Communist dictatorships eliminated most personal freedoms and gave ordinary people little voice in their government. Relations between Western countries generally improved, whereas relations among the Eastern European nations of the Soviet bloc and the West deteriorated.

Personal Freedoms
Making Comparisons
Recommended Use: Chapter Introduction
BL

Russian Casualties

Strategy and Activity

The Soviet Union lost between 20 and 30 million civilian and military people during World War II and was not eager to see Germany unified and strong, posing a threat once again to Russia. Remind students that past Russian history with Germany played a large role in Russia's actions during the Berlin crisis. Students should also understand that Berlin was the capital of Nazi Germany. It was divided into four spheres of influence immediately following the war, as described in the text. During the 1948–1949 crisis in Berlin, the Soviets blocked all entry into West Berlin, but the Allies chose not to give up the city to the Soviets. Instead, they air-lifted supplies to the 2.5 million people living in West Berlin. This airlift continued for about 10 months.

Russian Casualties
Identifying Central Issues
Recommended Use: Classroom Discussion
OL

Domino Theory
Comparing Time Periods
Recommended Use: Discussion Starter
OL

Domino Theory
Strategy and Activity

Have students compare the decision of the United States to enter the war in Korea with its decision to send military forces to Vietnam. What relationship might exist between these decisions? How did events in Europe after World War II support the U.S. belief in the domino theory?

Headed for a Fall
Comparing Time Periods
Recommended Use: Writing Assignment
OL

Headed for a Fall
Strategy and Activity

Have students write a brief description of the similarities between the fall of Napoleon III after his defeat in 1870 and Kruschev's problems after the Cuban missile crisis of 1962. Pose this question to the students as the basis for the assignment: "Were these defeats the actual reasons for these leaders' falls, or were they only an excuse and opportunity for people who already wanted to replace these leaders with others?"

Internet Learning
Bay of Pigs—40 Years After

The following site contains declassified documents from both sides of the conflict (Cuba and the United States) as well as audio recordings of conversations between President John F. Kennedy and his brother, Attorney General Robert F. Kennedy. Some documents were previously classified *confidential, secret,* or *top secret.* Documents were released at an international conference in Havana, Cuba, in March 2001. www.gwu.edu/~nsarchiv/bayofpigs/

In the Words of de Gaulle
Determining Meaning
Recommended Use: Group Activity
OL

In the Words of de Gaulle
Strategy and Activity

Write the following quotation, which is attributed to Charles de Gaulle, on the board or on an overhead transparency. "Only peril can bring the French together. One can't impose unity out of the blue on a country that has 265 different kinds of cheese." Organize the class into groups and have them discuss the meaning of this quotation. Group members should work together to interpret the meaning of de Gaulle's words. Remind students to support their thoughts with specific examples from this Chapter and previous ones. What historical examples can they find of unity and disunity in France? After a consensus is reached in each group, have group members share their results with the rest of the class. The entire class should then reach a consensus on the meaning of the quotation.

Development of Canada—An In-Depth Activity

Development of Canada
Interdisciplinary Connection:
Language Arts
Skill: Analyze Literature
Recommended Use: Team-Teaching
Strategy
AL

Background

Canada had a strong export economy based on its abundant natural resources. Then, after the war, Canada began developing electronic, aircraft, nuclear, and chemical engineering industries on a large scale. Investment of capital from the United States led to U.S. ownership of Canadian businesses. Some Canadians feared American economic domination of Canada. Canadians also worried about playing a secondary role politically and militarily to the United States. Canada established its own identity in world politics and government. It was a founding member of the United Nations in 1945 and joined the North Atlantic Treaty Organization (NATO) in 1949. Under Lester Pearson, the Liberal government created Canada's welfare state. A national social security system (the Canada Pension Plan) and a national health insurance program were enacted.

Strategy

Ask students to turn to page 1124 in Glencoe Literature's *The Reader's Choice: World Literature* to read "Spring over the City" by Anne Hébert, translated by Kathleen Weaver. While Hébert is best known for her novels, the Canadian author published her first book of poetry at age 26. After the death of her close cousin, poet Hector de Saint-Denys Garneau, Hébert's poetry developed a darker tone. She used powerful imagery and symbolism to explore controversial issues in Quebec provincial society. Explain to students that this sample of Hébert's writing is not overtly political; rather, it describes the transformation of Quebec City that is facilitated by the arrival of spring. Quebec is renowned for its winter snowfall and outdoor sports. Summer transforms it into a water-lover's paradise. Spring is the transition that carries winter out in its waterways and ushers in summer.

> Winter veers and tears like a flaking scale, the world is naked under
> bitter lichens
> Under masses of mud, old season, old papers, old cigarette stubs, old
> deaths flow in the stream . . .
> Now the season of waters draws back; the city dries like a beach, licks
> its wounds that taste of iodine
> Spring burns along grey façades and the leprous stones in the sun
> have the splendid shine of naked, victorious gods.

Hébert's use of figurative and sensory language (veers and tears like a flaking scale, licks its wounds, taste of iodine, spring burns) creates a vivid picture for the reader. Her use of repetition (old) and alliteration (stones, sun, splendid, shine) add a distinct musical quality to her writing.

Activities

Ask students the following questions, and then have them complete the activity below.

1. Compare and contrast your thoughts about spring to those expressed by Hébert in this poem. *(To some, spring comes gently and softly. In this poem, spring's emergence seems almost warlike.)*

2. What is implied in the last line? *(The city's structures have overcome winter.)*

3. **Writing Prompt** Ask students to write a poem describing their image of spring. Encourage them to incorporate figurative and sensory language.

CHAPTER 28

THE CONTEMPORARY WESTERN WORLD

Key Terms and Reinforcement
Strategy and Activity

Compile a list of key terms for this chapter. Include words such as:

détente	Thatcherism
dissidents	budget deficits
perestroika	gender parity
ethnic cleansing	postmodernism
autonomous	

Ask students to complete a word web. Demonstrate for students the structure of a word web that includes the following components:

- word history
- related words
- synonyms
- antonyms
- part of speech
- dictionary definition
- original sentence using the word
- how the word relates to the chapter

As students encounter the word in the text, they should add to their word webs the sentence from the text that uses the word. Supply college-level dictionaries, thesauri, and word origin dictionaries. Provide a model of the word web, using an overhead projector.

Key Terms and Reinforcement
Independent Practice
Skill: Use Word Webs to Analyze Important Terms
Recommended Use: Reinforcement
OL

Long on Tanks, Short on Refrigerators
Strategy and Activity

The Soviet emphasis on production of heavy industrial goods resulted in a shortage of consumer goods throughout the Soviet sphere of influence. Do students believe the people of Eastern Europe would have been more tolerant of the Soviet presence in their countries if they had enjoyed a better standard of living? Encourage students to consider what makes them more comfortable—knowing that the country has plenty of weapons to protect itself from attack, or having their consumer needs met.

Long on Tanks, Short on Refrigerators
Understanding How Policies Affect the General Populace
Recommended Use: Cross Curriculum—Economics
OL

Rival Nations
Strategy and Activity

Long before the advent of communism, the nineteenth-century French observer of American society, Alexis de Tocqueville, envisioned that the United States and Russia would one day dominate the world as rivals. Have students determine if they believe that Russia is still a rival or threat to the United States based on current policies of both nations. Have students support their inferences with factual information from newspapers, radio, or television reports they might paraphrase, or Internet articles that they can download. Ask students to present their analyses to the class.

Rival Nations
Making Predictions
Recommended Use: Group Activity
OL

Space Products
Research a Topic
Recommended Use: Enrichment
BL

Space Products
Strategy and Activity

Among the products developed as a result of the space race are super glue, Velcro, and a new form of glass. The first two are readily available and used daily, while the third is not yet marketed because the U.S. government purchases all of it for use in spy satellites. Have students conduct outside research to compile a more extensive list of commercial contributions derived from the space program. For example, most families probably have heat-resistant glassware cooking utensils that can withstand very high and direct-flame or heating-element temperatures. These commercial products were developed as a result of research into materials to protect vehicles from the intense heat of reentry into Earth's atmosphere.

Learn More About . . .
American Entertainment

The Cold War years had an influence on 1950s American entertainment as seen in the popular fad of horror films. Films, such as *I Came from Outer Space, The Thing, It Conquered the World,* and countless other thrillers, warned of deadly aliens coming to take over and destroy the United States and the world. Many Americans feared that was exactly what the Soviet Union planned to do. During the 1970s, Cold War tensions were temporarily relaxed and films such as *Close Encounters of the Third Kind* and *Star Wars* had non-threatening aliens and people from other planets that looked just like Americans. But the end of the 1970s began a "Second Cold War" and the entertainment industry once again reflected American fears. Science fiction films, such as *War Games,* and television movies, such as *The Day After,* dealt with the threat of nuclear world war.

Overload
Analyzing Key Concepts
*Recommended Use: Cross Curriculum—
Economics*
EL

Overload
Strategy and Activity

Write the following basic economic definitions on the board or use an overhead projector to display them:

Communism—a theory advocating elimination of private property
Capitalism—an economic system characterized by private or corporate ownership of (capital) goods

Then organize students into groups and have them create lists of reasons why conversion from communism to capitalism created economic problems in the states of Eastern Europe. Why would it be difficult for people to adopt the concept of the profit motive typical to capitalism? Point out that another aspect of the Communist system was that the state owned and controlled both the production of goods and their distribution. A capitalistic system is based on *private* production of goods and competition to gain a share of the market. The two systems are almost diametrically opposed with one system (communism) discouraging competition and innovation, while the other (capitalism) is based on both. Under a capitalist system, a person usually has many options, whereas the Communist system may offer only one. Thus, it would be hard for those emerging from communism to capitalism not to suffer "overload." Also, because competition was almost nonexistent, the work ethic in Communist nations was quite different from that in capitalist nations, where workers profit from their own individual efforts.

The Polish Revolution—An In-Depth Activity

Background

When Mikhail Gorbachev decided the Soviets would no longer send troops to support governmens of the satellite countries, revolutions broke out throughout Eastern Europe. Poland was one state where workers' protests led to demands for change. In 1980 a worker named Lech Walesa organized a national trade union known as Solidarity, which gained the support of workers and the Roman Catholic Church. Even when Walesa was arrested, the movement continued. Finally, in 1988, the Polish regime agreed to free parliamentary elections—the first free elections in Eastern Europe in 40 years. A new government was elected, ending 45 years of Communist rule in Poland.

Strategy

Ask students to turn to page 1009 in Glencoe Literature's *The Reader's Choice: World Literature* to read "Encounter" by Czeslaw Milosz, translated by the author and Lillian Vallee. Point out that the author was born in what became Poland after the fall of the Russian Empire. During the Nazi occupation of Poland, he remained in the country, participating in the resistance movement as a writer calling for freedom. After World War II, the Polish government appointed him to positions in the foreign service. By 1951 he could no longer ignore the abuses of the Communist regime, and he defected to the West, choosing to live and write in exile rather than in Poland under Russian domination. While Milosz has written many superb descriptions of landscapes, he draws a sharp distinction between an attachment to one's homeland and extreme forms of nationalism that promote ethnic hatred. He also refuses to idealize nature, as he accuses many American writers of doing. Ask students if Milosz's philosophy is evident in this poem:

> We were riding through frozen fields in a wagon at dawn.
> A red wing rose in the darkness.
>
> And suddenly a hare ran across the road.
> One of us pointed to it with his hand.
>
> That was long ago. Today neither of them is alive,
> Not the hare, nor the man who made the gesture.
>
> O my love, where are they, where are they going
> The flash of a hand, streak of movement, rustle of pebbles.
>
> I ask not out of sorrow, but in wonder.

Milosz is often described as a philosophical poet because of his interest in the nature of existence and identity. In 1980 he won the Nobel Prize in Literature.

The Polish Revolution
Interdisciplinary Connection: Language Arts
Skill: Analyze Literature
Recommended Use: Team-Teaching Strategy
AL

Activities

Ask students the following questions, and then have them complete the activity below.

1. Interpret the last line of the poem. *(The speaker may be wondering about the purpose for existence, or perhaps he is wondering about what happens after life ends.)*

2. Who is the "we" in the poem? To whom is the narrator speaking? *(Perhaps the author and his father or grandfather; the phrase "O my love" leads one to believe it is probably his wife or lover.)*

3. **Writing Prompt** Ask students to research a topic they believe represents an injustice in American government. Ask them to use the opinions and conclusions they draw from the research to write a politically motivated poem. Encourage the students to use either stark or allusive language.

LATIN AMERICA

Key Terms and Reinforcement
Strategy and Activity

Compile a list of key terms for this chapter. Include words such as:

multinational corporations	contras
magic realism	cooperatives
privatization	cartels
trade embargo	

Ask students to complete a word web. Demonstrate for students the structure of a word web that includes the following components:

- word history
- related words
- synonyms
- antonyms
- part of speech
- dictionary definition
- original sentence using the word
- how the word relates to the chapter

As students encounter the word in the text, they should add to their word webs the sentence from the text that uses the word. Supply college-level dictionaries, thesauri, and word-origin dictionaries. Provide a model of the word web, using an overhead projector.

Key Terms and Reinforcement
Independent Practice
Skill: Use Word Webs to Analyze
Important Terms
Recommended Use: Reinforcement
OL

Reason for Resentment
Strategy and Activity

Ask students to explain why Latin American women might be willing to take jobs that have low pay, long hours, and unhealthy working conditions. Why might these workers resent American attempts to encourage Latin American governments to force improvements in working conditions? A larger question to consider is whether Americans have any right to impose their standards on countries whose social and economic advancements for workers are many years behind those that workers in the United States fought to attain. Students should also consider cultural differences between Latin America and the United States.

Reason for Resentment
Understanding Differences
Recommended Use: Discussion Starter
OL

Dictators Come, Dictators Go
Strategy and Activity

Organize the class into groups of five to eight students. Provide the class with two scenarios in a Latin American nation. In the first scenario, a dictatorial leader has achieved power and is exterminating an entire ethnic group within the nation. Thousands are seeking asylum in the United States. In the second scenario, a Communist leader has achieved power and has nationalized all the industrial and agricultural interests of the nation. For both scenarios, the groups must decide whether or not the United States should help a faction within the nation remove its leader. Each group must review the viable options (do nothing, provide equipment and funding covertly, or provide overt military aid) and determine a course of action. Those groups that choose to do nothing must also consider the political, economic, and diplomatic repercussions of their choice. When the groups have completed their work, have them share their results, including the rationales that led to their decisions. Guide students in a general class discussion on the choices.

Dictators Come, Dictators Go
Role-play
Recommended Use: Cooperative Learning Activity
OL

Internet Learning
Latin America Online

The following site is a gateway to study a large number of Latin American countries with subjects from agriculture to sociology. www.lanic.utexas.edu/las.html

Absence Makes the Heart Grow Fonder
Understanding How Memories Affect Perceptions
Recommended Use: Chapter Wrap-Up
OL

Absence Makes the Heart Grow Fonder
Strategy and Activity

Ask students if they believe it is possible for the memory of a deceased leader to have a larger effect on a nation than the actual leader does. Evita Perón was the wife of the president of Argentina for six years, but many people believe her greatest legacy to her country is not what she did but in the way she is remembered. Ask students if there is a president of the United States whose memory has also been glorified beyond his actual achievements. Students may suggest President John F. Kennedy, but regardless of what president they select, they should be ready to support why they feel the memory is more endearing or more heroic than the actual life and achievements of the person.

People & Places
Castro

In its early phase, Castro's revolutionary regime was moderate. Gradually, however, its policies became radical and confrontational. Castro improved living conditions for Cuba's citizens but did not keep promises to hold elections. Thousands of middle-class and professional Cubans left the island after it became clear that a Communist revolution was under way. Ask students which of Castro's actions most probably resulted in U.S. determination to oust him as leader of Cuba. *(Soon after Castro's regime began to receive aid from the Soviet Union and arms from Eastern Europe, the United States broke off diplomatic relations with Cuba. When Castro openly avowed Communist principles, the breach could never be healed.)*

Gain or Pain?
Focusing on Economic Alliances
Recommended Use: Cross Curriculum—Economics
OL

Gain or Pain?
Strategy and Activity

Have students list reasons economic alliances can be both good and bad for a country's national interests. Nations of Europe may benefit from economic union, but they will also give up economic sovereignty. Why are some nations hesitant to join such alliances as the European Union or to adopt the euro as the common currency? The United States participates in an economic alliance—NAFTA—with its contiguous neighbors, based on furthering free trade among its members. Ask students if they think this arrangement could ever lead to a multination currency such as the euro. Why or why not?

The Mexican Way—An In-Depth Activity
Background

The Mexican Revolution at the beginning of the twentieth century created a political order that remained stable for many years. The official political party of the Mexican Revolution—the Institutional Revolutionary Party, or PRI—came to dominate Mexico. Every six years, leaders of the PRI chose the party's presidential candidate, who was then elected by the people. During the 1950s and 1960s, steady economic growth led to real gains in wages in Mexico. At the end of the 1960s, however, students began to protest Mexico's one-party government system. On October 2, 1968, university students gathered in Mexico City to protest government policies. Police forces opened fire and killed hundreds. Leaders of the PRI grew concerned. The next two presidents, Luís Echeverría and José López Portillo, made political reforms and opened the door to the emergence of new political parties. Greater freedom of debate in the press and universities was allowed. Economic troubles, however, would soon reappear.

Strategy

Ask students to turn to page 1103 in Glencoe Literature's *The Reader's Choice: World Literature* to read "The Window" by Jaime Torres Bodet, translated by George Kearns. Point out to students that Torres Bodet was not only one of the great writers to emerge from Mexico, but he was also director general of the United Nations Educational, Scientific, and Cultural Organization from 1948 to 1952. As such, he promoted educational programs throughout the world. Torres Bodet also served as a diplomat and Mexico's minister of foreign affairs. He felt that his governmental assignments kept him involved with the concerns of people, thus making him a better writer. Influenced greatly by the French literature his mother read to him as a child, Torres Bodet's writing displays elements of French movements, such as surrealism, or French writers and artists downplaying the importance of rational thought and questioning the very nature of reality. In "The Window," Torres Bodet considers isolation and writes:

> You closed the window. And it was the world, the world that wanted to enter, all at once . . . and now will never call to you again as it called today, asking your mercy! . . .

> But you were afraid of life. And you remained alone, behind the closed and silent window, not understanding that the world calls to a man only once that way. . . .

Critics and scholars have noted that Torres Bodet's poetry often expresses a "desire to overcome man's isolation in the twentieth century."

Activities

Ask students the following questions, and then have them complete the activity that follows.

1. Does this poem discourage isolation? Explain. *(Yes. It points out all that will be missed and accuses the listener of being afraid and naïve, not understanding that sometimes opportunity occurs but once.)*

2. Consider Torres Bodet's commitment to education and give an interpretation of this poem connected to education. *(Literacy provides opportunities to explore the world through reading or the knowledge to promote one's station in life. Perhaps this poem is an invitation to read and to learn.)*

The Mexican Way

Interdisciplinary Connection: Language Arts
Skill: Analyze Literature
Recommended Use: Team-Teaching Strategy
AL

3. Writing Prompt Ask students to write a letter addressed to a type of person they think would benefit from reading "The Window." Ask them to include poignant lines from the poem in their letter to emphasize the reasons they thought this person should read this poem.

Differentiated Instruction for the World History Classroom

AFRICA AND THE MIDDLE EAST

Key Terms and Reinforcement
Strategy and Activity

Key Terms and Reinforcement
Independent Practice
Skill: Use Word Webs to Analyze
Important Terms
Recommended Use: Reinforcement
OL

Compile a list of key terms for this chapter. Include words such as:

apartheid   Pan-Arabism
Pan-Africanism   intifada

Ask students to complete a word web. Demonstrate for students the structure of a word web that includes the following components:

- word history
- related words
- synonyms
- antonyms
- part of speech
- dictionary definition
- original sentence using the word
- how the word relates to the chapter

As students encounter the word in the text, they should add to their word webs the sentence from the text that uses the word. Supply college-level dictionaries, thesauri, and word-origin dictionaries. Provide a model of the word web, using an overhead projector.

People & Places
The Fear Factor

Ask students to evaluate the impact of international terrorism on their personal lives. Have they lost any freedom as a result of terrorist threats? Strict airport security is probably one of the most obvious effects. Students with family members in the military may be able to offer additional examples, as may those with international backgrounds. Another effect is the fear of international terrorism clearly seen in the immediate aftermath of the 2001 attacks on the World Trade Center and the Pentagon. Ask students if they are more fearful of potential terrorist activities after these attacks and if they think heightened security, especially at airports, will help protect against future attacks in the United States or elsewhere in the world.

Internet Learning
Nelson Mandela

Direct students to the following URL, which explores Mandela's long struggle against apartheid and for independence in his homeland. www.anc.org.za/people/mandela

AFRICA AND THE MIDDLE EAST

South Africa and Apartheid

Interdisciplinary Connection: Language Arts

Skill: Analyze Literature

Recommended Use: Team-Teaching Strategy

AL

South Africa and Apartheid—An In-Depth Activity

Background

European rule had been imposed on nearly all of Africa by 1900. However, after World War II, Europeans realized that colonial rule in Africa would have to end. In the late 1950s and 1960s, most black African nations achieved independence. In South Africa, where whites dominated the political system, the process of achieving independence was complicated. Blacks began organizing against white rule and formed the African National Congress (ANC) in 1912. Its goal was economic and political reform. The ANC's efforts, however, saw little success. At the same time, by the 1950s, South African whites (descendants of the Dutch, known as Afrikaners) had strengthened the laws separating whites and blacks. The result was a system of racial segregation known as apartheid ("apartness"). Blacks began demonstrating against these laws. The white government brutally repressed the demonstrators. After a long struggle, the government of F.W. de Klerk agreed to hold South Africa's first democratic national elections in 1994.

Strategy

Ask students to turn to page 151 in Glencoe Literature's *The Reader's Choice: World Literature* to read "The Prisoner Who Wore Glasses" by Bessie Head. Bessie Head was born in a South African mental hospital because her mother, an upper-class white woman, had been declared insane after she allowed herself to become pregnant by a black stable hand. Head grew up in a foster family and eventually moved with her son to Botswana to escape apartheid. A South African refugee once told Head about a group of prisoners who managed to make a prison officer more humane. She developed that account into "The Prisoner Who Wore Glasses." This is the story of 10 black political prisoners, called Span One, who were grouped together for convenience sake. Prison regulations stated that "no black warder should be in charge of a political prisoner lest this prisoner convert him to his view." The unity created by this arrangement "never seemed to occur to authorities [to be the source of] strength of Span One and a clue to the strange terror they aroused in the warders." Thus, Span One "got out of control. They were the best thieves and liars in the camp." This group of men acted as they chose to act, with Brille, one of the "prisoners who wore glasses," as one of the ringleaders. When Warder Hannetjie is placed in charge of Span One, things change. He seems to have "eyes in the back of his head" and catches Brille eating cabbages and stealing grapes. Essentially, it seemed for two weeks that "Span One as a whole was in constant trouble." Then a pivotal event occurs—Brille catches Hannetjie "in the act of stealing five bags of fertilizer and he bribed me [with tobacco] to keep my mouth shut." Thus, a new relationship develops between Span One and Hannetjie, with the guard "slipping off his revolver and picking up a spade to dig longside Span One" and Span One "stealing certain commodities like fertilizer which were needed on the farm of Warder Hannetjie."

Activities

Ask students the following questions, and then have them complete the activity below.

1. How is this a story of survival? *(Unlikely people cooperate to meet their needs in a bad situation.)*

2. How is Hannetjie a dynamic character? *(He learns to respect the intelligence and cunning of the political prisoners. He treats them humanely, and they respond in turn.)*

3. **Writing Prompt** Ask students to write an essay explaining a time they cooperated with someone, not necessarily because they liked the person but because it was in their best interest to cooperate. Ask students to include their original reasons for dissent and how their cooperation altered the situation.

CHAPTER 31

ASIA AND THE PACIFIC

Key Terms and Reinforcement
Strategy and Activity

Compile a list of key terms for this chapter. Include words such as:

communes	discrimination
permanent revolution	occupied
per capita	state capitalism
stalemate	

Ask students to complete a word web. Demonstrate for students the structure of a word web that includes the following components:

- word history
- related words
- synonyms
- antonyms
- part of speech
- dictionary definition
- original sentence using the word
- how the word relates to the chapter

As students encounter the word in the text, they should add to their word webs the sentence from the tsext that uses the word. Supply college-level dictionaries, thesauri, and word-origin dictionaries. Provide a model of the word web, using an overhead projector.

Work, Work, Work
Strategy and Activity

Assign students to describe their own conception of the term *work ethic*. Do they believe American workers always perform to the best of their abilities at work? Will they stay late at work if a job is not finished? Do they take the success of the firm they work for as a sign of their own success? In what ways do firms encourage their workers? Ask students to explain how social or cultural values such as a strong work ethic have helped Japan become an economic success. Can students identify and explain any "downside" to these values? Do they believe these values are likely to last in the long run? Do Japanese workers have a stronger work ethic than workers in the United States have? Do work ethics change over time?

Internet Learning
Vietnam: Yesterday and Today

Direct students to the following URL where they will find information and additional Web site resources to enhance their study of Vietnam.
www.servercc.oakton.edu/~wittman/

Key Terms and Reinforcement
Independent Practice
Skill: Use Word Webs to Analyze
Important Terms
Recommended Use: Reinforcement
OL

Work, Work, Work
Compare and Contrast
Recommended Use: Classroom
Assignment
EL

The Vietnam War

Interdisciplinary Connection: Language Arts

Skill: Analyze Literature

Recommended Use: Team-Teaching Strategy

AL

The Vietnam War—An In-Depth Activity

Background

In Vietnam, leading the struggle against French colonial rule was the local Communist Party, led by Ho Chi Minh. In August 1945, the Vietminh, an alliance of forces under Communist leadership, seized power throughout most of Vietnam. Ho Chi Minh was elected president of a new republic in Hanoi. Refusing to accept the new government, France seized the southern part of the country. For years, France fought Ho Chi Minh's Vietminh for control of Vietnam without success. In 1954, after a huge defeat at Dien Bien Phu, France agreed to a peace settlement. Vietnam was divided into two parts. In the north were the Communists, based in Hanoi; in the south were the non-Communists, based in Saigon. Both sides agreed to hold elections in two years to create a single government. Instead, the conflict continued. The United States, opposed to the spread of communism, aided South Vietnam. In spite of this aid, the Viet Cong, South Vietnamese Communist guerrillas supported by North Vietnam, were on the verge of seizing control of the entire country by early 1965. In March 1965, President Johnson sent U.S. troops to South Vietnam to prevent a total victory for the Communists. North Vietnam responded by sending more forces into the south. By the 1960s, there was a stalemate. After reaching an agreement with North Vietnam in 1973 in the Paris Peace Accords, the United States withdrew. Within two years, Communist armies forcibly reunited Vietnam.

Strategy

Ask students to turn to page 747 in Glencoe Literature's *The Reader's Choice: World Literature* to read from *When Heaven and Earth Changed Places* by Le Ly Hayslip. Explain to students that when the author was 12, her village was overrun with Viet Cong and soldiers fighting for the South Vietnamese government. At 13, Hayslip joined the Viet Cong's children's troop and fought for three years against U.S. and South Vietnamese soldiers. During the war, Hayslip was imprisoned and tortured by South Vietnamese soldiers and then was sentenced to death by the Viet Cong as a suspected traitor. She escaped to the United States where she found a new life. This excerpt from *When Heaven and Earth Changed Places* described Hayslip's early relationship with her father who was "built solidly—big-boned—for a Vietnamese man, which meant he probably had well-fed, noble ancestors." After Hayslip's brothers and sisters leave home—the brothers to fight and the sisters in search of a better life—Hayslip's father, a nontraditional Vietnamese man to begin with, realizes the importance of his only child left at home and begins to educate Hayslip about her ancestry. He tells her of a distant female ancestor who gave birth and continued to fight against the ancient Chinese Han. He emphasizes that Hayslip was worthy of her example, telling her to follow in this ancestor's footsteps. Eventually, Hayslip's father explains to her the devastation wrought on the family because of the war against France and the Vietnam War. He charges Hayslip to "stay alive—to keep an eye on things and keep the village safe. To find a husband and have babies and tell the story of what you've seen to your children and anyone else who'll listen. Most of all, it is to live in peace . . . ."

Activities

Ask students the following questions, and then have them complete the activity below.

1. How is this a story of survival? *(The father recognizes the need to preserve the history of his people.)*

2. What is Hayslip's job? *(Her job is to preserve the family history, promote peace, and bear children.)*

3. **Writing Prompt** Ask students to interview members of their family to collect stories of the family history. Ask students to record the stories they collect in writing for future generations and to share one story aloud with the class.

CHAPTER 32

CHANGING GLOBAL PATTERNS

Key Terms and Reinforcement

Strategy and Activity

Compile a list of key terms for this chapter. Include words such as:

ecology	bioterrorism
deforestation	global economy
desertification	peacekeeping forces
globalization	disarmament

Ask students to complete a word web. Demonstrate for students the structure of a word web that includes the following components:

- word history
- related words
- synonyms
- antonyms
- part of speech
- dictionary definition
- original sentence using the word
- how the word relates to the chapter

As students encounter the word in the text, they should add to their word webs the sentence from the text that uses the word. Supply college-level dictionaries, thesauri, and word-origin dictionaries. Provide a model of the word web, using an overhead projector.

Key Terms and Reinforcement
Independent Practice
Skill: Use Word Webs to Analyze Important Terms
Recommended Use: Reinforcement
OL

The American Century

Strategy and Activity

The twentieth century has often been called the "American century" because of U.S. dominance as a military and economic superpower. Many people from other parts of the world still have concerns that U.S. cultural dominance will one day "Americanize" the world, overwhelming their own society's traditions. Professor Benjamin Barber of Rutgers University wrote that in the modern world, "fast music, fast computers, and fast food—MTV, Macintosh, and McDonalds . . . are pressing nations into one commercially homogeneous global theme park, one McWorld tied together by communications, by information, by entertainment, by commerce." His fear for this new "McWorld" is that it may become one where democratically minded citizens are replaced by dollar-oriented consumers. Ask students if they think this can happen in the twenty-first century and what might be the results in democratic nations if this did occur. Ask students who have relatives or friends in other countries to contact them via e-mail to obtain and share with the class a foreigner's opinion on whether "Americanization" is good for their country.

The American Century
Compare and Contract
Recommended Use: Chapter Wrap-Up
OL

What Do I Wear?
Understanding Global Interdependence
Recommended Use: Research
BL

What Do I Wear?
Strategy and Activity

Assign students to survey the clothing they own to find what percentage of it was manufactured in the United States and what percentage was imported. There are labels on most clothing that provide this information. Have students bring this information to class to share. It is likely that they will find most of their clothing was imported. Guide students in a discussion of life in a global economy. What would happen to the quality of their lives if the United States did not trade with other nations? Would they be able to find the products they want to buy at the prices they are willing to pay?

Protection, Preservation, and Policy
Understanding Global Alliances
Recommended Use: Class Discussion
OL

Protection, Preservation, and Policy
Strategy and Activity

Solving the problems of today's highly interdependent world requires coordinated problem solving among nations. At the same time, nationalist sentiment among small groups makes cooperation difficult. Guide students in a discussion of the role that organizations such as NATO, SEATO, OPEC, and the UN play in coordinating solutions to international problems. These alliances have varying original purposes, including military protection (NATO and SEATO), economic protection (OPEC), and diplomacy (UN). Have students identify the full names of each of these organizations. Do students feel that these groups may contribute to international problems? If so, how? NATO was formed in 1949; SEATO in 1954; OPEC in 1960; and the UN in 1945. Can and do organizations or alliances outlive their usefulness? Have these associations changed to adapt to the worldwide shift away from a military mindset to a technological one? If so, how? Is the United States a member of all these alliances?

Global Challenges and Global Visions
Interdisciplinary Connection: Language Arts
Skill: Analyze Literature
Recommended Use: Team-Teaching Strategy
AL

Global Challenges and Global Visions—An In-Depth Activity
Background

Since 1945 tens of millions of people have migrated from one part of the world to another. There are many reasons for these migrations. Persecution for political reasons caused many people from Pakistan, Bangladesh, Sri Lanka, Eastern Europe, and East Germany to seek refuge in Western European countries. Brutal civil wars in Asia, Africa, the Middle East, and Europe led millions of refugees to seek safety in neighboring countries. Most people who have migrated, however, have done so to find jobs. Latin Americans seeking a better life have migrated to the United States. Guest workers from Turkey, southern and eastern Europe, North Africa, India, and Pakistan have entered more prosperous Western European lands. In the 1980s and 1990s, foreign workers often became scapegoats when countries faced economic problems. Political parties in France and Norway, for example, called for the removal of blacks and Arabs in order to protect the ethnic purity of their nations. In Asian countries, there is often a backlash against other Asian ethnic groups.

Strategy

Ask students to turn to page 1129 in Glencoe Literature's *The Reader's Choice: World Literature* to read "When Greek Meets Greek" by Samuel Selvon. Point out to students that although governments tend to consider global issues from a broad perspective, individuals within a society have a responsibility to promote global unity on a smaller scale. Intolerance and racial prejudice are serious issues of individual and global concern, and as a writer who often wrote about West Indian immigrants to the United Kingdom, Selvon (who was of Indian descent) explored this theme in many of his works. "When Greek Meets Greek" tells of Ram, an immigrant to London from the West Indies. While searching notice boards for a place to rent, Fraser, a contact man (someone who has useful information that is not common knowledge), tells Ram about a room for rent, but the landlord has vowed not to take any renters from the West Indies. To increase his chances of getting a room, Fraser encourages Ram to impersonate an Indian from India by wearing a turban when he sees the racist landlord. Ram refuses to wear the turban, but tells the landlord he is from India. While conversing with the landlord, an Indian tenant, dressed in traditional garb, passes. Ram, under pressure, attempts to greet the Indian in the native language but calls out different types of ethnic dishes instead. He is surprised when Mr. Chan, the Indian tenant, seems not to notice. While Ram secures a room, he finds himself greatly worried that Mr. Chan will discover his real identity. In the process of trying to get Mr. Chan evicted in order to alleviate his worry, Ram's nationality is revealed, and he is evicted. Ram sees Fraser and complains about Chan. Ironically, Fraser informs Ram: "Man, that is a fellar from Jamaica who I send to that house to get a room!"

Activities

Ask students the following questions, and then have them complete the activity below.

1. What message is Selvon sending through this selection? *(Racism is shallow.)*

2. Why did Ram refuse to wear a turban? *(He was uncomfortable pretending to be something he was not. Even though he claimed to be from India anyway, perhaps wearing the turban was taking things too far in Ram's mind.)*

3. **Writing Prompt** Ask students to write an essay explaining one way they can contribute to racial or ethnic unity in their school, community, state, or country.

DATE DUE